THE
CUSTOMER
OF THE
FUTURE

BLAKE MORGAN

THE CUSTOMER OF THE FUTURE

10 GUIDING PRINCIPLES FOR WINNING TOMORROW'S BUSINESS

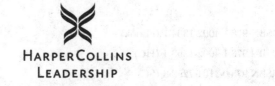

HarperCollins
Leadership

AN IMPRINT OF HARPERCOLLINS

Published by HarperCollins Leadership, an imprint of HarperCollins Focus LLC.

Any internet addresses, phone numbers, or company or product information
printed in this book are offered as a resource and are not intended in any
way to be or to imply an endorsement by HarperCollins Leadership, nor does
HarperCollins Leadership vouch for the existence, content, or services of these
sites, phone numbers, companies, or products beyond the life of this book.

Book design by Pauline Neuwirth, Neuwirth & Associates.

ISBN 978-1-4002-1364-1 (eBook)
ISBN 978-1-4002-1363-4 (HC)
ISBN 978-0-3101-7259-8 (SC)

Library of Congress Control Number: 2019944463

For my parents, Debra Malschick and Dr. Michael Landau. For the blood, sweat, and tears of parenting. For all the effort, all the love, and giving me the opportunity to dream big.

CONTENTS

ACKNOWLEDGMENTS

I'd like to thank my husband, Jacob Morgan, who—with his own career success—has taken me with him, who was never too busy to listen to me practice my speeches, read my manuscript, or bounce ideas around. Thank you for pretending to love all the "investments" I make in my keynote speech wardrobe, for doing dishes, and for changing diapers—for being a wonderful father to our little girl. The biggest decision of my life was choosing you almost ten years ago, and it was the best. Having a family of our own has been the experience of a lifetime.

My daughter, Naomi, there is nothing like a hug from a three-year-old that makes you remember what is important in life. Thank you for letting me love you and not crying when I have to leave for an airport. You really are a dream come true.

Thank you to my editor, Tim Burgard, who took a chance on me. Thank you for your encouragement, patience, and simply being an advocate for me even when I decided to scrap the first version of this book idea. A shout-out to Franklin Goldberg, who responded positively to my LinkedIn request asking for an introduction to HarperCollins. Thank you to everyone who I interviewed in this book, who kindly answered my many questions. Thank you to the folks at Amazon and Sephora, who spent a lot of time answering my questions, so I could get your stories right in this book.

I'd like to acknowledge my clients, who give me the opportunity to be the keynote speaker at their conferences. I'd also like

ACKNOWLEDGMENTS

to thank the many people online whom I engage with and whom I have never met in person but who listen to *The Modern Customer Podcast*, read my *Forbes* column, watch my YouTube videos, comment on my LinkedIn posts, and are generally nice to engage with. Thank you to my team who help me reach more people.

I'd also like to thank you—the reader—for being interested in this topic and choosing to spend time with me to dive deeper into it.

THE
CUSTOMER
OF THE
FUTURE

INTRODUCTION

> The only constant in life is change.
> —HERACLITUS OF EPHESUS[1]

In the permanent darkness of the caves in the lower Rio Grande, a translucent fish thrives. This albino-looking cave dweller is not different than any other fish, except for the fact that the fish is blind. However, this fish was not always blind; the entire species of this fish *became* blind over time. Living in a dark cave with little oxygen, finding food is difficult. When living in darkness, eyesight is not helpful and being efficient is critical to survival. Over time, these fish sacrificed their eyesight so they would be able to retain more energy to find food and survive in the difficult environment of the caves; the blind fish have 15 percent more energy than eye-seeing fish.[2] These small pinkish miracles are called Mexican Tetra.[3] They evolved as their dark and uncertain environment required. They did not go into a cave and die; they learned to thrive in the cave by losing the sight that was useless to them in that environment.

The blind cave fish remind us that it's our ability to evolve, adapt, and embrace change that determines our ability to survive in the world. It is no different for the businesses we create and run.

Some days when I go into my local grocery store in Northern California and buy freeze-dried mangoes that were picked from a tree in Thailand, I stop in wonder. I stare at the miracle of modern life for humans, where we can get almost anything, anytime, from anywhere. It's a miracle that many of us take for granted.

Today, comfort has become the status quo. Most of us don't have to think about an early death from an outbreak such as the black plague.[4] If someone boarded a ship to another country a hundred years ago, you likely never saw them again. But today with the click of a button you can communicate on video or text with anyone in the world. Modern life is astonishing when you think about how far we've come. But those blessings brought by technology come at a price. Keeping up with constant advances and the complexity and disruption they come with is no small task. In a recent survey of international business school graduates, the top threat facing global business leaders was the pace of technological and digital advancement surpassing the current churn of economic, political, and environmental changes.[5]

We are blind to the future and unprepared for it, much like the Mexican Tetra is blind to its cave world. Unlike the blind cave fish, humans are programmed to resist evolution. We fight change. We want to stay safe and cozy. We want to imagine that we do not need to change in order to continue to thrive. The reality is, nature is working against us. Our bodies have a complex internal system that purposefully creates inertia—resistance to change—to maintain a state of equilibrium known as homeostasis. This helps the human body maintain a normal body temperature, metabolism, weight, and other functions necessary for survival.[6]

In the last few years, we have seen unprecedented disruption to the business world. Some of the entities we believed in disappeared overnight, like ghosts. We stood by, shocked, and then continued to enjoy alternative options in our own lives. Only fifty-three of the companies on the Fortune 500 list in 1955 were still on the list in 2018.[7]

With all of this disruption happening, how can a company stand out? It turns out that how we make people feel has a significant impact on their perception of us: that is, customer experience. For example, Apple has always differentiated its products with experience. The products are engineered beautifully; however, it's not just the product that customers love, it's also the constant improvements made to the phone. In fact, a recent survey found Apple's iPhone to have twice the customer loyalty rate as the next highest brand. In my last book I intended to set the record straight on customer experience because I was tired of people simply throwing the phrase *customer experience* in the same bucket as *customer service.* That made no sense to me. In my book *More Is More: How the Best Companies Go Farther and Work Harder to Create Knock-Your-Socks-Off Customer Experiences* I defined customer experience as the perception the customer has of a brand. Perception is not always reality, but increasingly as individuals and as businesses, we must be aware of how we are making people feel.

A study by McKinsey found that 70 percent of the customer's journey is dictated by how the customer feels they are being treated.[8]

If you are reading this book, you have a human body: that body has a nervous system tasked with the physiological processing of emotion.[9]

For example, joy can fill our entire bodies, giving us the desire to jump for joy or break out into dance. Happiness can be exhibited with laughter. In fact, studies have been done to show which parts of the body various emotions affect, including organs, muscles, and limbs. When we feel nervous or anxious, it can impact our stomach or our chest.[10] We feel frustration when we are unable to fulfill our needs; continued frustration results in anger, depression, loss of self-confidence, annoyance, aggression, or worse.[11]

As humans we have emotional and physical reactions to our environments. When we build experiences for other people, we must be conscious of how we make other people feel. We need insights into the reality of how customers experience our products and services, not how we hope they would experience them. Today we can gain greater insight into how we make people feel through data, through analytics, and via other methods. These methods will gain traction as the market becomes more crowded, and customers have an increasing number of options.

I have spent ten years studying and in some ways championing this topic, which only now seems to have reached a level where it is reverberating throughout the business world. Research shows that a moderate increase in customer experience generates an average revenue increase of $823 million over three years for a company with $1 billion in annual revenues.[12] Small improvements in efficiencies can accumulate into significant impact. Today, customers have choice, and they prefer to work with companies that make their lives easier and better. Indeed, 62 percent of consumers believe that the best brands succeed in making their lives easier.[13] Sometimes customers want to feel special and other times they want to achieve a task or solve a problem so simply that the interaction is almost invisible. Customers are willing to spend more money with companies that make them feel good than with companies that make them feel bad or frustrated. The payoffs of great experiences include a 16 percent price premium (18 percent in the US) on products and services, plus increased loyalty.[14]

If you read this book this year, or in five years, there will continue to be one constant—the rate of change is increasing. Sustaining continual change requires a different mindset. We must think like blind cave fish, willing to let go of methods and approaches that have served us well in the past but are no longer working. In this book, I have studied the latest research on customer experience and interviewed leading companies and executives who excel at customer experience. My ten guiding principles will give you the tools you need to create complete strategies to create experiences for the future customer. Going through a customer experience transformation will require hard work. It will require focus and resources. I want you to be successful, and I want to inspire at least one idea that impacts how you evolve your business and helps you survive and thrive.

The solution to customer experience is rather simple, but not easy. The challenge is this—most companies are product-focused rather than customer-focused. This lack of a customer experience mindset is the reason customer experiences are varied and often fall short. Most businesses have an internal-looking view: when they make decisions, they make them because it is better for their own bottom line—the short-term value of their own company. When a company is product-focused, they do not have the mindset required to level-up the customer experience. It becomes visible over time through company culture, behaviors, and actions—and these things impact customer satisfaction, customer loyalty, and sales. In chapter 1, we look at what a customer experience mindset looks like in action, and how you can create it. I take you through my own experiences visiting Amazon and Sephora, both companies that embody a customer experience mindset.

In chapter 2, we take that customer experience mindset one step further and consider the customer-centric culture. Companies today cannot begin to think about creating superior customer experiences without getting their own house in order first. In chapter 2, we talk about companies with a strong company culture; we look at the latest research on employee experience and the ties between a healthy company culture and your bottom line. After examining the attributes of a customer-centric culture, we'll learn more about the next key step in creating a customer-focused company: leadership development.

A development program that trains leaders to be transformational leaders can make or break your customer experience program. In chapter 3, we explore the traits and habits of today's most transformational leaders. Too many companies believe one executive can turn around a company. The best companies have leadership development programs in place that develop the leaders they need for tomorrow. Leadership development is operationalized.

After the discussion of mindset, culture, and leadership in chapter 4, we start getting into the topic of designing customer experiences that are thoughtful and consider how customers actually experience products and services. Chapter 4 explores the role of efficiency and constant innovation in the pursuit of creating a desirable, zero-friction customer experience.

From a discussion of zero-friction customer experiences we move into the discussion in chapter 5 of how to build marketing for the customer of the future. We look at the CMO (chief marketing officer) of the future and how they need to be as much a strategist as anyone else on the C-suite. We consider the content habits of generation Z, and how marketers need to be thinking about the values of this socially aware generation. From our discussion of marketing in chapter 6, I unpack today's customer experience technology landscape, and distill the most important strategies for your customer experience management technology approach. We look at the impact of artificial intelligence on customer experience and the emergence of the cloud.

In chapter 7, we dive into digital transformation, and I provide you with a modern definition of digital transformation as it relates to customer experience. In chapter 8, we look at the role of personalization in the modern customer experience, and explore recent compelling examples of personalization. We look at the new landscape of direct to consumer, and how these new D2C models have become successful leveraging innovative approaches to customer acquisition and engagement. In chapter 9, we move on to a discussion of analytics and consider a new approach to customer lifetime value. We'll also look at new forms of predicting customer behavior and identifying key patterns in behavior with predictive analytics.

We close with chapter 10, where we discuss key considerations in privacy and data ethics. Artificial intelligence requires a new approach to managing customer data, and in this chapter we consider ethical questions for every company today.

This book should inspire at least one key idea you can immediately use at your own company. I have spent years combing the planet for the best approaches to creating better experiences for other people. I care deeply about your experience reading this book, and as you read it I encourage you to send me notes and feedback, or talk to me about an idea that has inspired you. I also encourage you to assess how customer-focused your organization is by taking my *Customer of the Future* quiz for the book at www .CustomerFutureQuiz.com. You can contact me directly as you read this book at blake@blakemichellemorgan.com.

CUSTOMER EXPERIENCE MINDSET

> If there's one reason we have done better than our
> peers . . . it is because we have focused like a laser
> on customer experience.
> —JEFF BEZOS[1]

Customer experience has become a front-and-center conversation across the world. In fact, 72 percent of businesses say that improving the customer experience is their top priority.[2] Brands that have superior customer experience bring in 5.7 times more revenue than their competitors.[3] Customer experience is a big differentiator, and three trends are behind how this has come to be: the rise of the experience economy, a power shift from the company to the customer, and advances in technology that allow us to create more powerful customer experiences.

While price and quality are still the top considerations for consumers making a purchase decision, in one study 73 percent of respondents said that a good experience is key in influencing their brand loyalties.[4] Providing an experience around a product or service is a smart investment. Companies that differentiate on experience find ways to make the customer's life easier or better, to make the customer feel special, or to wrap a story around the product. One cannot simply throw up a product that is identical to thousands of other products and expect to be successful.

Today we live in a world where YOLO ("you only live once") drives purchasing decisions for generation Z (born between 1998 and 2016), as well as millennials (born after 1980). Consumers increasingly value experiences over things, powering the experience economy. By 2020, generation Z will account for 40 percent of all consumers.[5]

Part of what is driving the experience economy is the desire to curate digital lives, which you will read more about in this chapter. In one study, nearly 20 percent of generation Z respondents said they have stayed at a specific hotel or destination in order to score a positive response from followers on posts on their own social media channels.[6] Up to 71 percent of generation Z would get a part-time job to save up for a leisure trip.[7]

Millennials are also saving their money for interesting experiences. More than three in four millennials would choose to spend money on a desirable experience or event over buying an attractive product, and 55 percent of millennials say they're spending more on events and live experiences than ever before.[8] Recent research from Dr. Thomas Gilovich suggested that people find more lasting happiness investing in experiences over buying things.[9] The study found experiences are the glue of our social lives. Experiences enhance social relations, form a person's identity—even a bad experience makes for a great story to share via social media.

A recent example of how this trend translates into business is LVMH—a luxury retailer we'll talk more about later in this chapter—which recently purchased luxury travel company Belmond with plans to make traditional luxury travel less about opulent hotels and accommodations and more about one-of-a-kind experiences.[10] They realize modern consumers care more about creating an Instagramable memory than purchasing the hottest new product. Brands like T-Mobile and Casper also are creating showrooms where customers can experience the product, make a memory, and buy something if they desire. But how did we get here, to a time where people would rather save up for an exotic trip, participate in a compelling adventure, or learn a new skill with friends over buying a thing?

In 2008, the stock market crashed, the worst financial crisis since the Great Depression in 1933. I was living and working in New York City at the time, at a conference company, and I will never forget how quiet the streets were. Restaurants once filled with patrons were completely empty. This crisis in the subprime mortgage market in the United States became a global full-blown banking crisis with the collapse of the investment bank Lehman Brothers.[11] The same year, an investor named Bernie Madoff—whose firm was one of the top market makers on Wall Street—was found to have operated the biggest Ponzi scheme in history, a form of fraud that gives the illusion of a sustainable business.[12] Prosecutors estimated the size of the fraud to be almost $65 billion.

Millennials—today the largest living adult generation—were watching as their career plans were disrupted. Young people who went to school to become bankers or lawyers found the jobs had vanished. Their parents and grandparents lost their 401(k) plans or retirement savings. Young people learned that wealth could disappear in a moment's notice.

The things that had defined their parents' and grandparents' lives were not going to be the main achievements of millennials' lives. More young people opted to live in cities. Millennials opted to focus on their own aspirational dreams, putting off marriage, homeownership, and kids.

I say all this without mentioning the enormous innovation happening in tandem with these events: the internet and the proliferation of the smartphone—which armed 2.5 billion people (as of 2019) with a small computer in their pocket.[13] People were now able to broadcast their lives online. Social media played a big role in enabling young people to create an identity online.

This leads us to modern life, where many people choose to spend their money on experiences over things. According to

McKinsey, consumers of all ages are opting for experiences, with millennials—the largest-spending group today—spending the most.[14] Lifecasting has become a popular activity, and people curate their digital footprints with extreme focus and care. Facebook (created in 2004), YouTube (created in 2005), Twitter (created in 2006), and Instagram (created in 2010) ushered in a new era of curation and lifecasting, inspiring users to generate Instagramable content." The smartphone, in tandem with the viral growth of these social networks, played a critical role in getting us to this inflection point today.

The sharing economy democratized travel, empowering more people to explore the world at better prices. Airbnb launched an offering on their platform called "experiences" to "discover things the locals do." Airbnb advertises this offering as "activities designed and led by inspiring locals." They immerse guests in unique worlds.[15] Learn to bake with a famous pastry chef in Paris, take a dance class in Havana, Cuba, or get a photography lesson from an expert who will help you photograph the Sydney Opera House at sunset.

People want to feel something: they want to experience all that this world has to offer and they want to share these experiences with the world. Customer experience must be geared to this modern customer, who values experiences over things, and expects the businesses they frequent to empower and assist them as they navigate modern life.

THIS BRINGS US TO THE second trend driving the customer of the future: social media and the shift in power and influence from the corporation to the customer. Social media and smartphones armed customers with a platform and a microphone. Suddenly customers were talking about the experiences they were having, and companies were not prepared to engage with the customers. Companies thought social media would be a way for them to engage positively with customers, but customers expected brands on sites like Twitter and Facebook to help solve customer service issues for them. Companies were forced to engage with customers, expanding their social media teams and adding resources to serve customers on multiple channels.

Not only did customers demand companies help them with service needs, but they also had unprecedented power and an ability to share their responses to marketing campaigns. Companies faced backlash when they released ads that were perceived as racist, sexist, or offensive to groups such as veterans. Tone-deaf advertisements resulted in social media protests, and sometimes affected stock prices.[16] Companies struggled to engage in public discourse.

The business world expected social media to empower brands, but instead customers became empowered. Nearly three-quarters of millennials report that their perception of a brand improves when it is clear the company responds to customers' social media inquiries.[17] But brands were not accustomed to immediate feedback from customers (and from people on the internet who might not even be customers). Brands were required to respond and engage. Brands became more self-conscious of public opinion, now that it could travel fast and light a fire, which could bring down the company. From a customer service perspective, there has been a palpable shift in power from the brand to the customer. Social media forced brands to treat customers better, because the world was watching and they were now being held accountable.

THE THIRD TREND THAT SHAPES the current state of customer experience is technology. In the past, customer experience technology was an "above-and-beyond" customer relationship management tool, but today having a customer relationship management tool is table stakes. Technology has empowered businesses to create efficiencies and meet the needs of a new era of demanding customers. More than half of customers actively seek to buy from the most innovative companies.[18] We are seeing exponential growth in technology: Over the last five decades, the number of transistors (the tiny electrical components that perform basic operations) on a single chip have doubled regularly. This is the reason a modern smartphone packs incredible capability into such a small package.[19] Connectivity has proven to be a critical aspect of modern life: Whether they're in a rice paddy in China or on a cruise off the coast of New Zealand, people expect to be connected to the internet, and able to communicate with their family and friends. There are more than 5 billion unique mobile users in the world today, up 100 million (2 percent) in the past year. They all expect to have connectivity wherever they go.[20]

The cloud—which we will talk more about in chapter 6—has made data storage incredibly easy and affordable. Every company today is a technology company. Increasingly, we're seeing companies call that out—like Allstate, an insurance company that now calls itself a data and technology company.

Technology increasingly shapes customers' most beloved customer experiences. In a survey of 15,000 consumers, 73 percent of respondents said they value companies that offer up-to-date technology through customer experience.[21] Technology allows companies to provide zero-friction, seamless customer experiences. Many of these companies are digital natives that deeply value the importance of digital innovation. According to *Fortune*, five of the top ten "most admired companies" are technology companies, including Apple, Amazon, Microsoft, Netflix, and Alphabet (Google). Most brands are reliant on a few key technology companies.[22] Even Netflix—which competes with Amazon's content services—relies on Amazon to host its content in the cloud through Amazon Web Services.[23] Advances in machine learning and artificial intelligence have enabled a new era of automation, of robots, and of personalization. Companies can do much more with data than they ever could before, not only gaining insights on the past, but also predicting the future—enabling them to better anticipate customer needs, gain real-time feedback, optimize pricing, identify customer flight risk factors, staff up or down, or make real-time marketing bets. In a 2018 survey of US senior decision-makers, big data and analytics was listed as the most important emerging technology for enhancing the customer experience.[24]

Customers today get consumer-grade technology experiences in their personal lives, enjoying the use of social media, apps, and Apple products. Consumer-grade technology is what you experience with apps that are seamless. Customers expect the same frictionless experiences from the companies they do business with. Companies today are scrambling to digitize and are focusing on digital transformations, better leveraging technology to solve all kinds of problems with efficiencies, logistics, and supply chain. Companies are in a race to make life easier and better for customers—and they are starting by creating efficiencies for employees. By focusing on issues like logistics and supply chain, companies are better able to get customers products faster, and create more personalized customer experiences. In chapter 7, we will look at digital transformation and how companies can do it right. A study at MIT found that companies that have embraced digital transformation are 26 percent more profitable than their peers.[25]

COMPANIES THAT DO CUSTOMER EXPERIENCE WELL

Imagine you work at Amazon. You are sitting in a meeting with Jeff Bezos and thirty others. It's around the holiday season and Bezos wants to check in on customer service. On this particular morning he wants to know how long customers have to wait on hold with the call center. Bezos throws the question over to Bill Price, VP of customer service. The VP assures Bezos that customers wait on hold for less than a minute to talk to a person in the contact center. Bezos thinks about it for a second and responds,

"Really? Let's see." He takes his phone out, dials Amazon customer service, and enables speaker. One minute, then two minutes, then three minutes, then four minutes pass—and Bezos is still on hold with customer service. He is visibly angry. Thirty executives sit holding their breath as this embarrassment unfolds. It takes four and a half minutes for Bezos to get through to an Amazon call center agent. The VP of Customer Service resigns shortly after this happens.[26]

For a company that has a reputation for being a hard-core place to work, Amazon will go to any length for the customer. Bezos knows waiting is a mood-killer for customers. And while most companies don't use customer feelings as a KPI (key performance indicator), it seems that Amazon does. Amazon is unapologetic about the actions it takes to provide value to customers. I don't see any other company with the singular focus on customer experience I see from Amazon.

Very few companies have this customer experience mindset. The question is: Are you product-focused or are you customer-focused? A customer experience mindset is when every decision at the company is made based on what is best for the customer. A product mindset is when a company makes decisions based only on what will increase profitability for the company, without thought for who it impacts.

Feelings are not a hard business metric. But increasingly the most innovative companies take feelings very seriously. In a study of 1,000 consumers it was found that 65 percent of respondents felt they had an emotional bond with a brand. Technology, fashion, and lifestyle brands were among the most likely to build a strong emotional connection with their customers.[27]

Recent research from the *Harvard Business Review* suggests the most empathetic companies increased their financial value far more than less empathetic firms.[28] Empathy has never been in more demand. Amid continued economic and political uncertainty around the globe, simply asking, "What does it feel like for the person on the receiving end of this experience?" is a major differentiating factor for companies. If word is out that customer experience investments can bring a return, why don't more companies do it well? Simply put, it's hard. Many companies surveyed by Worldwide Business Research claim that execution is the biggest obstacle to implementing a customer experience improvement strategy.[29]

Companies are short-term thinkers, and they are not willing to sacrifice short-term profits for long-term value. We know that Amazon bled millions of dollars for many years before becoming profitable, but most companies are not willing to make that trade-off.

In one interview in this book, an executive told me that you should overmanage the things you care about, a page from Disney's book. It turns out customer experience is created and impacted by the guts of your organization. It can be messy to start digging around and looking for efficiencies, rewiring your company. Although it is necessary, most companies are not willing to take the time and resources to go through this surgery.

I WENT TO AMAZON MYSELF, AND THIS IS WHAT I FOUND

Whether you think Amazon is the greatest company on earth or the most evil company on earth, they are building the most customer-centric company on earth.

You cannot talk about customer experience without talking about Amazon because they have changed the game for every single business on the planet. Amazon's e-commerce sales in the US are up 30 percent from a year ago, expected to reach $258.2 billion this year. Amazon captured nearly half of the US e-commerce market by the end of 2018.[30]

Whether you think Amazon's internal practices are wonderful or terrible, what they are doing is working. Amazon's core retail business continues to grow while it dominates the cloud-computing market and is gaining rapid adoption of its Alexa voice assistant in the home. Amazon's workforce has increased in the last eight years to over 600,000 employees. Its stock price has more than quadrupled since 2013. Amazon caters to the customer that seeks a frictionless, on-demand, and personalized customer experience. Amazon's personalized recommendation system generates 35 percent of all sales for the company.[31]

In November 2018, I had the chance to go to Seattle and visit Amazon for myself. I have written about Amazon for years, and been a customer since 2009. I was expecting some kind of magic show. But instead I met caring, humble, hardworking, and thoughtful people.

I was in a group of six authors, thought leaders, and professors on an Amazon influencer symposium. We had many chances to ask Amazon executives questions in intimate meet and greets. I posed a question to one longtime senior Amazon executive: "Who owns customer experience at Amazon?"

I was curious if he would mention a chief customer evangelist or chief marketing officer. But he was confused and I had to repeat the question for him. It turns out everyone—literally everyone—owns it. The thought of making one single person responsible for millions of customers seemed ridiculous and impossible. That person would be a figurehead and nothing more.

AMAZON CULTURE IS CUSTOMER-OBSESSED, AND all executives reflect this focus. Amazon employees are told not to concern themselves with external rumors or gossip. Bezos said once in an employee meeting, "Look, you should wake up worried, terrified every morning . . . but don't be worried about our competitors because they're never going to send us any money anyway. Let's be worried about our customers and stay heads-down focused."[32] Bezos, the richest man on earth, recently said that he doesn't believe Amazon is "too big to fail." He said, "In fact, I predict one day Amazon will fail. Amazon will go bankrupt. If you look at large companies, their life spans tend to be thirty-plus years, not a hundred-plus years." He added, "The key to prolonging that demise is for the company to 'obsess over customers' and to avoid looking inward, worrying about itself."

He said, "If we start to focus on ourselves, instead of focusing on our customers, that will be the beginning of the end. . . . We have to try and delay that day for as long as possible."

Being focused, and having a customer experience mindset, is a tool that Amazon uses. What are employees focusing on? At most companies you would find that focus is across the map. Marketing is focused on getting as many eyeballs as possible, sales is focused on getting the most sales, and customer service is focused on solving as many customer issues as possible while cutting costs for the company. At Amazon everyone would tell you the same thing: They are building the world's most customer-focused company.

Focus is a behavior driven by goals; key performance indicators that employee performance is measured by. With companies being siloed, often these KPIs are all over the map. Frequently KPIs are not tied to customer experience, and as a result there is no single focus at the company.

Goals matter. The goals of the company matter. Broken down, the goals of business divisions matter, and the goals of the teams working in those divisions matter. To take this a step further, the goals of the individual employee matter. They accumulate to create a company culture, a mindset.

When I walked the halls of Amazon's Fulfillment Center B414, famous for Kiva robots that move equipment, I read the many signs all over the building: "Start with the customer and work backward. We work vigorously to earn and keep customer trust." And, "Pay attention to competitors but obsess over customers." And lastly, "We consider the customer in everything we do."

In an organization there is often so much chaos and noise, and it is not clear what the focus should be. Sometimes work doesn't seem to be about work at all—it's about simply not drowning in corporate culture. If employees are busy playing politics or navigating bureaucracy, they lose the ability to focus. Today's business environment is cutthroat. If all of your energies are not focused around a common goal, you risk being bulldozed by a more agile company, an Amazon.

If you want to adopt a customer experience mindset, like Amazon does, you can do the following:

- Create a set of leadership principles to live by.
- Ask employees to consider if every decision is product-focused or customer-focused.
- Evaluate your KPIs, and consider if these are driving customer experience–focused behaviors in your teams or not.
- Ensure every team is aligned around a common goal, and that the goal is tied to customer experience.
- Consider if your leadership is customer-focused or not, and if not, find out why and try to fix it (without getting fired).

AT TIMES BEING CUSTOMER-FOCUSED IS BRUISING

If you read about Amazon's early days, to say the culture was tough is an understatement. But like any big company the experience of employees at Amazon varies a great deal depending on the team and the boss. While there has been criticism of the culture in the past, this is not the experience of everyone. Amazon has topped many "great places to work" lists. I personally know someone who took a job with Amazon, specifically for the work-life balance, to be home by 5:00 p.m. with her kids.

To change the world takes incredible discipline—and perhaps this is why Amazon hires so aggressively from the military—because these are people used to demanding and challenging conditions. Hate Amazon or love them, they are persevering. They are completely changing consumer behavior, and forcing every other company to rise to the occasion: Everyone is comparing the experience you offer to that of Amazon.

Bezos once told author Brad Stone, "If you want to get to the truth about what makes us different, it's this. We are genuinely customer-centric, we are genuinely long-term oriented, and we genuinely like to invent." Bezos went on to say that most companies are focused on the competitor, rather than the customer. He said that companies want to work on things that will pay dividends in two or three years, and if they don't work in two or three years they will move on to something else. "They prefer to be close followers rather than inventors, because it's safer."

WHY OTHER COMPANIES DON'T HAVE THE MINDSET

For many decades customer programs within companies have struggled to achieve any kind of reputation other than as a cost center. Call centers are notorious for cutting resources, measuring how much time agents take to answer a customer's question, even measuring how long of a bathroom break an agent takes. Why is it that one company comes along and decides to become the world's most customer-centric company and creates a $1 trillion market cap for itself, while others stand on the sidelines watching Amazon gobble up more and more market share?

The answer is profits. Most CEOs are brought in to make a company more profitable. Studies show the longer a CEO is in the role, the lower the return to shareholders.[33] New CEOs tend to be more open to change and gain more returns. The average S&P 500 CEO tenure length has fallen to five years.[34] They must make the board happy by increasing the value of the company, and after doing their job the CEO is free to move on to their next

CEO job, with a pay raise. The CEO is routinely measured by quarter-to-quarter success. So why on earth would you go against the grain and invest in something that would take three to five years to see the benefit of?

While the CEO is often seen as setting the tone for the company, CEOs come and go. The leadership of the company needs to be resilient and stable, rather than relying on one person to shape the company's mindset. It's important to have a leadership development program that trains executives at all levels, but the program needs to be customer-centric, and stronger than simply one executive who is brought in to change everything. Turnarounds require a team effort. (We'll talk more about leadership development in chapter 3.)

If a company does not have a culture where the customer is at the heart of everything the company does, it is harder to achieve this customer focus later in the company's existence. If the goal of your company has been to simply make increasing amounts of money, that is not an inspiring goal for the individual employee.

If a company wants to achieve a goal, they have to embrace the mindset to achieve it, but you can't force a mindset on employees. When senior executives embrace the mindset, everyone else will mirror their behavior. If executives only care about sales, then you will have employees who only care about sales.

In his 1954 book, *The Practice of Management,* Peter Drucker wrote that the purpose of a business is to create a customer.[35] But to modernize Drucker's statement we could say the purpose of a business is to make a customer's life easier and better. To expand that, the purpose is to remain relevant in the customer's life by continuing to find ways to be of service to the customer.

At the beginning of the chapter, we heard that Jeff Bezos believes one day Amazon could disappear. There is a sense of humility in the way he talks; he is earning his company's existence every single day. Most businesses do not have this sense of humility. For businesses, the obvious goal is to make money—otherwise you don't have a business. The problem with focusing on the money is you are skipping a step; you are only focusing on the end result.

In a recent survey of CEOs, 40 percent said their top priority was growth, 15 percent said money, and 10 percent said sales.[36] The focus has to be on the journey—on what it takes to create a business where people continually want to buy from you. This seamless, personalized, zero-friction customer experience offered by Amazon makes other customer experiences pale in comparison, and the customer experience mindset is the reason Amazon can move as quickly and powerfully as it does.

SEPHORA: CUSTOMER EXPERIENCE MINDSET IN ACTION

Amazon started as an internet company, but it's also informative to look at a company that started as a retailer, and evolved to become a data and technology company. Sephora has established a modern identity as a customer experience–focused company that uses every technology and data tool in its arsenal to create a powerful customer experience.

We've established in this chapter that every company has a mindset, and that mindset results in a focus for an individual employee. But often that individual employee focus is not connected to the customer experience: Most employees within a company never actually see or talk to a customer. However, in some companies, the customer remains the heart of everything the company does. At Sephora, the company is agile, quickly adapts to change, and employees are organized around a common goal. Like Amazon, the company does not have one person that owns customer experience; it's woven throughout the fabric of the entire company. Everyone works together to create and nurture that mindset.

Sephora is a beauty retailer that opened in 1970. The company's founder, Dominique Mandonnaud, wanted shopping to be a unique and fun experience. Sephora's "assisted self-service" sales experience was different than the traditional retail models for cosmetics. In 1997, Sephora was purchased by LVMH, which also owns Louis Vuitton and a total of sixty subsidiaries. Sephora was an early player in e-commerce, launching its website in 1998. The company was struggling in 2003 and LVMH almost sold it but instead brought in Jacques Levy, a CEO who set Sephora on a trajectory for continued growth. The company focused on customer preference, realizing their competitive advantage was in the fun and playful shopping experience they built their legacy on. They crafted a new purpose statement, "To provide customers with the most entertaining shopping experience of the retail industry—giving them a moment of relaxation and discovery, enabling them to experiment and play with their beauty."

Today the company has 2,300 locations in thirty-three countries. At a time when social media has exploded, and consumers want to look camera-ready as they post to Instagram, YouTube, and everywhere else, Sephora has been by the consumer's side, making her look like any other reality TV celebrity. I am a loyal Sephora customer, and the makeup you see in my photo on this book jacket was done at Sephora by a Sephora makeup artist. (The makeup applications are free with the purchase of $50 worth of makeup.) These services make Sephora popular with customers, bringing luxuries like a makeover to anyone with the purchase of a few products. As we talked about earlier, the Experience Economy is not simply about selling a product, but providing a service around the product customers cannot get anywhere else.

The company has always had a customer experience mindset, but when they decided to go through a transformation, executives knew it would require a shift in thinking, structure, and hiring. Sephora employees aim to think like customers—asking themselves, "How would I want to shop, what would make my experience better, how do my kids' interactions with technology predict the future?" The teams then brainstorm.[37] Technology has always been a focus for Sephora and today the company elevates digital to the C-level by having a head of omnichannel retail. According to LVMH, "Sephora achieved sustained growth across all areas of operation. With omni-channel at the heart of its strategy, online sales advanced rapidly."[38]

LVMH saw 11 percent organic growth in the first half of 2018, thanks to growth in North America and Asia. The expansion and renovation of its distribution network is continuing with a new store concept in China and the first Sephora-branded store in Russia.[39] At the heart of Sephora's aggressive growth strategy stands the customer, who simply wants to look and feel better: Sephora is customer-centric, not product-centric.

Sephora was recognized as one of the world's most innovative companies by *Fast Company* in addition to being named "Retailer of the Year" by the World Retail Congress in 2018. The company is committed to hiring a senior leadership team that is largely female because that reflects their female customer base. The company is not shy about its mission: "Sephora believes beauty is for each person to define, and for them to celebrate. They support and encourage bold choices in beauty—and in life. Their purpose is to inspire fearlessness." They don't simply support customers, they focus on supporting employees. The company has become known as a "mecca for female tech professionals." The Sephora Innovation Lab, which launched in the San Francisco headquarters in 2015 with a team of five women leaders, was built to test new technologies for Sephora stores, Sephora.com, and digital advancements including the Sephora App, Sephora Virtual Artist, Digital Makeover Guide, and much more. Sephora customers are often women, so it makes sense that those building the actual experiences for these female customers are also women.

Having a customer experience mindset is not easy, or everyone would have one. The mindset takes a deliberate shift from a product-focus to a customer-focus. Sephora has this mindset and it's made Sephora one of the most competitive beauty companies in the world.

MAKE THE CUSTOMER THE
FOCUS OF EVERYTHING YOU DO

I will never forget the fall day I visited San Francisco to meet with Sephora's Chief Technology Officer, Ali Bouhouch. The air was filled with smoke from the devastating Northern California fires as I took the ferry into the city. I did my makeup with Sephora products and then wore a special mask over my face and under my sunglasses. I was nervous that the CTO would not be going into work because of the air, but the office was full. When I met with him, I wanted to talk about technology, but he quickly shifted the conversation to the customer. Bouhouch told me there are two things to focus on in business: Put the customer at the heart of everything you do, and be in the business of relationships, not transactions.

Bouhouch was hired in 2015 when Sephora went through what they call a "strategic revision." His role would be to help Sephora go through a digital transformation to provide the most modern experience possible to the customer.

When we think of IT, we generally don't think about a customer experience mindset. We think of IT as a fix-it shop, like going to an internal DMV. But today's customer experience requires IT leaders to be innovators. Bouhouch told me he could have built the traditional CTO "elite think tank" with what he called a "thou-shall-follow attitude." But he did not do that. He spent the first ninety days on the job learning the business and listening to his business partners so he could build a thoughtful technology experience that was in step with the culture. He said he had to join with a humble attitude because he is not a consumer of Sephora products and had never worked in cosmetics. He also is looking at the broader landscape, because while he says businesses in other industries might not think they compete with the customer experiences offered by Amazon or Netflix, they do—because every customer is comparing their experiences with Amazon and Netflix.

Bouhouch told me he does not see the customer as simply a wallet. He's interested in the story of the customer: "If we build a relationship with a young lady who is struggling with acne, her struggle is her self-image." This customer might be searching for a product for her skin regimen that will clear up her acne in six months, but Sephora wants to help her feel more confident today. This means finding acne coverage she can walk out of the store with. Bouhouch said, "These are small installments to help her build self-confidence."

Sephora now offers social impact classes under Sephora Stands, supporting diversity and inclusion efforts, as many of Sephora's customers are part of the LGBTQA community. Sephora is "committed to providing these individuals with the tools they want to feel confident and beautiful every single day." Since the launch in 2017, Sephora's "Classes for Confidence" program has hosted over 1,500 classes and reached more than 8,500 people.

Sephora celebrates its diverse employee base and customer base, and ensures it carries lines that meet the needs of customers of all backgrounds. For example, it carries Fenty Beauty by Rihanna, the beauty line by musician and fashion icon Robyn "Rihanna" Fenty that caters to a variety of skin tones, with a lauded 40+ shade foundation range.[40] Upon its launch, Fenty Beauty by Rihanna sold out in Sephora stores, to customers who had long felt underrepresented in makeup and with no exact color match for their skin.[41]

Sephora inspires fearlessness in all kinds of ways, and shows its commitment to their customer no matter who that customer is.

EMPLOYEE EXPERIENCES AT SEPHORA

Sephora designs an inclusive employee and customer experience. What you notice when you walk into a Sephora retail store is the diversity of the staff. Employees look different: there might be a man teaching a class on contouring and people of all ages and body types doing makeovers and acting as greeters. For a recent holiday ad campaign, Sephora invited 11,000 North American employees to apply for inclusion. The final ads that were used during the holidays read "Let's beauty together."[42]

At Sephora, 92 percent of employees feel when they are hired they are made to feel welcome. And 90 percent said they are proud to tell others they work at Sephora. They have recently made the Great Place to Work Institute.[43]

When it comes to employees, what we measure matters. Most companies are tracking sales as a measure of success, but Sephora is tracking more than that. In my interview with the CTO, he said Sephora is tracking success by looking at revenue, customer loyalty, and employee satisfaction. For an ROI equation at a company, tracking employee experience is incredibly rare. But Sephora understands if you want to retain customers, you first must retain employees. They are one of the many companies who now recognize that having an employee-focused mindset is the first step in having a customer-focused mindset. Bouhouch knows you cannot force a culture: you can design one, but it also has to be emergent.

With a view of downtown San Francisco, during our Friday afternoon hour together, Bouhouch tells me, "Think of us as a Hollywood studio. We are building beauty experiences. We do the storyboarding and the casting." His employees are the "cast."

Even at its inception in 1970, Sephora was launched to make beauty more fun. Customers come to Sephora to learn, to try new things. It's not the same as when you go to a car dealership, and you can smell the snake oil on the car salesman. At Sephora the beauty advisors are not held to individual sales quotas—which makes them less aggressive and pushy than you might find in other makeup counters. (The entire store is rewarded for hitting a sales quota, but not individual beauty advisors, which empowers a team effort.)

If You Want to Be Inspired by Sephora's Customer Experience Mindset

- ▻ Think of your company more like a lab than a factory.
- ▻ Offer a service around your product to bring customers into your stores.
- ▻ Embrace diversity inside your company; hire and develop executives that match your customer base.
- ▻ Ensure your technology or IT shop sits down with the business to understand the needs of the business as well as the culture of the company.
- ▻ Take risks on new technologies to improve the customer journey.

In this chapter we've established what a customer experience mindset is, and we've looked at two different organizations—Amazon and Sephora—that embody this mindset. As we think about developing customer-focused leadership in chapter 3, I'd like you to keep in mind the mindset that these leaders of the future must create within the organization. Now we'll examine how to develop customer-focused culture, your first step in transforming to serve the customer of the future. From a discussion on culture we'll explore the role of leadership, and how customer-focused leadership will create the tailwind necessary to serve the customer of the future.

2

BUILDING A CUSTOMER-CENTRIC CULTURE

> Always treat your employees exactly as you want
> them to treat your best customers.
> —STEPHEN R. COVEY[1]

Companies often miss an obvious business strategy: the key to higher profits is employee experience. Companies that do employee experience well have 4.2 times the average profit of those who don't, according to a study of 252 companies.[2]

My own definition of culture is creating a space where people feel safe, where they are challenged to create personal growth, and that they want to come back to every day. If you—reading this book—feel great at work, then you are going to produce better work. If you feel a lack of purpose, you don't have the tools you need to do your job, and you are uncomfortable with working conditions, your work will suffer. Employee experience is the first step in creating a customer-focused culture. Many companies treat culture as an afterthought, particularly in the business to business space, where only 14 percent of large B2B (business-to-business) companies have a customer-centric culture.[3]

Culture is at times invisible. For Michael Stallard, author of *Connection Culture: The Competitive Advantage of Shared Identity, Empathy, and Understanding at Work,* the question is: How are you communicating an inspiring vision, valuing people, and giving them a voice?[4] He believes culture must be simple, actionable, and memorable. If you already have a culture established, you must always seek feedback from your employees on how that is going. Every day Amazon asks employees one question about how things are going at work. (You will read more about this in chapter 4.)

Culture is something you have to continually work at. As your company grows, and you work harder at your customer experience, you will need to train and develop managers who are responsible for their teams' experience at work.

A recent survey showed that 51 percent of CFOs say they play a role in shaping corporate culture. The most common ways they do that is by using company principles and values to guide actions (83 percent), contributing to the development of the company's mission (79 percent) and collaborating with other executives to define the desired culture (78 percent).[5]

If you can create a leadership strategy for your mid-line managers, you will do something most other companies never figure out. In a recent Gallup poll, it was found that managers account for at least 70 percent of the variance in employee engagement scores across business units.[6] When it comes to employee experiences, managers play a critical role in shaping everyday work experiences. According to Gallup, organizations with engaged employees outperform the competition by 147 percent.[7]

Scott Morris is a salesperson and employee at Workday, a software company in Silicon Valley that replaces a company's core record system for human resources (HR) and finance. He's also a dad. The software that Morris is tasked with selling is not an easy product to sell, and he was not selling much of it. The challenging part of software and technology sales is these software systems are replaced every ten to twenty years.

To add insult to injury, not only was Scott's career on the rocks but his daughter had been recently diagnosed with dwarfism and he realized Workday's employee insurance was not going to cover the extensive speech training his daughter would need.

Knowing how important the speech training was for his daughter, and the limits of his employer's insurance, Morris was thinking of throwing in the towel and leaving his company altogether. But before simply giving up, he approached human resources and asked if they would be willing to make an exception in the insurance policy for his daughter's coverage.

To his surprise, the improved insurance was granted. This was a turning point in Scott Morris's career at the company. After this incident something changed for Scott. He became an incredibly successful salesman. In the six months following, he secured three huge deals for the company, bringing on important new customers such as Target.

I was told this story at a dinner party by Greg Pryor, SVP of People and Performance Evangelist at Workday. We had simply started talking about the link between employee experience and customer experience. He had seen it for himself. When Pryor told me this story, he said Workday's chief human resource officer did not even recall approving the special request for Scott Morris (and was shocked to later find out Morris was a critical part of Workday's growth). That's how normal it was to simply do the right thing for employees. In 2012, Workday's IPO valued the company at $9.5 billion. The company boasts a 98 percent customer satisfaction rating.

This story of Scott Morris is a reminder that how we feel at work impacts the work we create. Many of us have many jobs that we do not get paid for, but are even more important than our actual job. Being a parent has changed me as a person at my core. I would do anything for my daughter, and I would never want to have to choose between a job I was passionate about and my daughter's healthcare. But these are hard decisions that other employees have to make every day. Workday can inspire other companies that want to commit to improving their employee experiences and reap the benefits of that improvement.

POP CULTURE REFLECTS A MODERN WORLD

Today's modern employee and customer require a new leadership style. A survey of more than 6,700 managers found that managers who show more empathy toward direct reports are viewed as better performers in their job by those managers' bosses. Being empathetic and vulnerable helps leaders better connect with their employees.[8]

In movies and TV shows about business in the past the sensitive businessperson was made to seem weak. The beloved TV series *Mad Men* featured confident tough guys. Many of us grew up watching movies like *Wall Street* or *Goodfellas* or *The Devil Wears Prada,* which also feature strong and sour personalities who you won't see in a vulnerable moment. Steve Jobs was famous for being a bully. Any movie ever made about Wall Street depicts arrogant, unsympathetic, and greedy bankers who call it like they see it.

But something has shifted, both in the content we watch and in the leaders we see thriving. Shows and movies made today depict men who are willing to be vulnerable. There are also more women and people of diverse backgrounds in leadership roles onscreen. In 2015, the hashtag #OscarsSoWhite went viral, a reaction to the lack of representation at the annual event. By 2019, the highest amount of Academy Awards were won by black women at the Oscars.[9]

Diversity is not just important for the media we consume; it's an important part of creating a customer-focused culture. Companies in the top quartile for racial and ethnic diversity are 35 percent more likely to have financial returns above their respective national industry medians, according to a study from McKinsey.[10]

Unfortunately, rather than seeing more diversity in business, we are seeing less. The number of female CEOs and CEOs of color in Fortune 500 companies has dropped in recent years.[11] Having diverse leadership representation can help your business. Companies that reported above-average diversity on their management teams also reported innovation revenue that was 19 percent higher than companies with below-average leadership diversity, according to one recent study.[12] As generation Z enters the workforce, they will demand more diversity in leadership. When presented with the statement "I have one or more friends who are of a different race than me," 81 percent of generation Z agreed, compared to 69 percent of millennials.[13] They want to work for companies that understand the importance of having a balance of people leading the organization.

When people complain that they don't have more women leaders or conference speakers or engineers because "they just can't find them," I find that a hard pill to swallow. Simply ask your employees. In the US, 47 percent of workers are women.[14] It is time that companies hire employees that reflect the diversity of the real world. In fact, women drive 70 to 80 percent of all consumer purchasing, through their buying power and influence.[15] Women are your employees and your customers.

Diversity in your leadership team means diversity of thought, and insights into a diverse customer base. According to recent research, transformational leaders tend to be more inclusive and lead more diverse teams.[16] People who don't listen, who can't read the room, and who aren't aware of the people and situations around them don't thrive in today's cultural climate. We live in a time where people are more socially aware. Recent movements like #MeToo and #BlackLivesMatter have caused employers to think more honestly about their own approach to leadership and human resources, and how supportive they are actually being of their people.

THE SKILLS, MINDSETS, AND COMMUNICATION STYLE OF THE MODERN LEADER

It's not just diversity that matters when it comes to hiring your leadership team. It's important to hire leaders with the right skills, mindsets, and even communication style. We live in a time when that macho leader or bully won't thrive any longer. Transformational leaders who know how to motivate a team and lean on the experts around them fare better than those who try to do everything alone. They foster a culture of collaboration where all types of employees interact, rather than high-level executives with high-level executives, and lower-level employees with lower-level employees. A study of fifty-five large teams found that one of the biggest factors in successful collaboration was support from leaders. The study found that teams do well when executives invest in supporting social relationships, demonstrate collaborative behavior themselves, and create what is known as a "gift culture." In this gift culture employees experience interactions with leaders and colleagues as something valuable and generously offered—as if given a gift.[17]

Not only are transformational leaders today good listeners, thoughtful, and willing to be vulnerable, but they are also more humble than in the past. CEOs talk directly to customers via social media. Take Elon Musk. He often thanks customers for their support of Tesla, and asks how the company can improve.

Elon Musk ✔ @elonmusk · 26 Dec 2017 ⌄
Wanted again to send a note of deep gratitude to Tesla owners WW for taking a chance on a new company that all experts said would fail.

So much blood, sweat & tears from the Tesla team went into creating cars that you'd truly love. I hope you do.

How can we improve further?

💬 17K   ♻ 14K   ♡ 142K   ✉

He even took a tip from a customer on Twitter who requested "dog mode" for the Tesla vehicle, which would keep the car comfortable for a dog waiting for its owner.

Comcast—which is digging its way out of a dark past with its customers—now understands the power of a customer-focused culture. CEO Brian Roberts and every executive in the company make two customer calls a month to learn about customer pain points and have authentic conversations about how Comcast can improve.

Amazon employees know if they ever get an email from their CEO, Jeff Bezos, which simply is a forward of an email a customer sent Bezos, they'd better fix the customer issue as soon as possible. Bezos gets email from customers (his personal email is posted online as Jeff@Amazon.com, and he ensures these customers get what they need by routing them to the right department).[18]

American Family Insurance CEO Jack Salzwedel was recognized as the world's most engaged CEO on Twitter. He's replied to customer queries eight times more and posted nearly a hundred times more than his colleagues.[19] John Legere, the CEO of T-Mobile, connects with customers by being approachable and authentic. Legere, who on T-Mobile's website is called the "Un-CEO," has a crockpot cooking show called #SlowCookerSunday. He also shows how customer-centric he is by responding to customer complaints and questions on Twitter, often within minutes.[20] Business leaders who thrive in today's environment are intuitive, emotionally intelligent, and willing to be vulnerable.

Employees who had managers with a high emotion quotient (EQ) were four times less likely to leave than those who had managers with low EQ.[21] Brené Brown—an expert on social connection—conducted thousands of interviews to discover what lies at the root of social connection. What she found is that a person's willingness to be vulnerable improves social connection, and social connection is a large part of what we get out of work.[22] As Erin Meyer, author of *The Culture Map*, puts it: "Leaders have always needed to understand human nature and personality differences—that's nothing new. . . . What's new is the requirement for twenty-first century leaders to be prepared to understand a wider, richer array of work styles than ever before and to be able to determine what aspects of an interaction are simply a result of personality and which are a result of differences in cultural perspective."[23]

If You Want to Create a Customer-Focused Culture

▶ Hire people who are emotionally intelligent leaders and managers.

▶ Hire a diverse set of leaders who reflect a diverse customer base.

▶ Normalize candid conversations to create a culture of transparency and open communication.

▶ Encourage leadership to spend time out in the field talking to customers.

▶ Ensure managers keep an open line of communication with employees, and managers are involved in building and developing an employee-centric culture.

▶ Talk to employees, and learn what employees like or don't like about the culture.

When you are focused on getting products and services in the hands of customers, a culture can be an afterthought. Simply put a poster on the wall, right? But whether they like it or not, a culture emerges.

Culture is shaped by people, and changes over time. What starts as a company focused on purpose, eventually becomes a company focused on operational efficiencies once its original founders leave. Companies must work to keep their vision alive through the company culture.

BEING CUSTOMER-FOCUSED IS HARD, AND CAN TAKE ITS TOLL ON EMPLOYEES

Companies that are customer-focused are often also employee-focused. However, if you are a customer-focused company, the standards are high. There is little room for error, and customer satisfaction is prioritized above all else. This can leave employees feeling burned out. I once gave a talk at a Fortune 500 company known for being both employee- and customer-centric. The talk I gave was about having the energy to influence change and step up for your customers. One executive came up to me after the talk and told me the employees were all texting each other during my session. I spoke about self-care and the importance of putting yourself first, and he felt my message was in conflict with the culture of the organization, where high expectations and high velocity demanded much from employees. This is a company that is often recognized for both employee experience and customer experience. Their stock price has increased 360 percent in the last five years. However, sometimes the demands of a customer experience and success can throw employee experience out of balance. Every company today must diligently work to keep the balance of employee experience with customer experience. If you demand too much from your employees, they will get burned out, and find jobs elsewhere.

Culture can be challenging when organizations are focused only on bringing the best experience to the customer. At what point do we stop focusing on the customer and think about the well-being of employees? A recent study carried out by the University of California Riverside found that companies offering employee wellness programs saw a gain in productivity among workers. Employees who participated improved productivity an average of one full workday per month.[24] A summary of seven cost analysis studies revealed a $3.48 return on investment for each corporate dollar spent on wellness programming.[25] For example, well-being plays a crucial role in multinational food company Danone's overall business strategy, which is based on the two pillars of economic and social growth. The company's Dan'Cares program provides medical coverage for most significant health-related risks, and the company has implemented a global parental leave policy. Danone wants their employees to be healthy, and act as health ambassadors that represent their food brand well.[26]

If Your Velocity Is Taking a Toll on Employees, Here's What You Need to Do

- Senior leadership should model self-care. Emails should not be sent at 2:00 a.m. or on weekends.
- Health and wellness programs for employees should be a focus at the company.
- Consider more flexible vacation policies. Encourage self-care and mental health days. Netflix has no vacation policy and simply asks employees to take vacation when they need it.
- Create guardrails, but grant freedom to employees so they can do what is best for the customer in the moment.
- Reward delegation and efficiency improvement ideas. Employees should be incentivized to collaborate and find ways to make their work smoother.

There is no one-size-fits-all for culture. What works for one company will not work for another company. You can't simply create a culture formula, and have that miraculously work. And in plain truth, sometimes brutal cultures—where employees are expected to go above and beyond—can push a company toward success. Start-up environments are often run by underpaid and sleep-deprived young people. Pulling off audacious dreams sometimes requires periods of brutality. I do not condone it, but this is sometimes what happens, so let's not sugarcoat it. But word has gotten out that the excitement offered by a start-up can wear off. The Economic Innovation Group surveyed 1,200 millennials and found that more millennials believed they could have a successful career by staying at one company and attempting to climb the ladder than by founding a new one.[27]

WORK IS ONLY ONE PART of a person's life. Many of us have various interests and facets of our lives. We have families, children, hobbies, health to take care of. We know that today there are already very few boundaries between work and life, particularly for knowledge workers who can be reached anywhere, anytime.

You cannot work people incredibly hard without repercussions, no matter how much they love their jobs and leaders. Relationships suffer when workers are being asked to work nights and weekends—they are stressed out and are not there for their spouses or children. When workers are stressed, their health can suffer. Lack of sleep is linked to accidents, depression, diabetes, heart attack, stroke, weight gain, and the list goes on.[28]

Customer-focused cultures are responsible and accountable to the customer, but not at the cost of the employee.

The best cultures are created by leaders who care about the well-being of their workers. Providing a flexible work environment will help create a more customer-focused culture. Not everyone works and focuses in the same way. Research shows 70 percent of employees feel distracted at work, with chatty coworkers and office noise as the top distractions. When workplace distractions are reduced, whether through training or policies, 75 percent of employees are more productive, 57 percent have increased motivation, and 49 percent are happier at work.[29]

I am introverted, and while as a younger worker I could make the open office plan work—I even enjoyed the social aspect of it when I was young—I don't anymore. I love working at home. When I worked at other companies, the attitude was "butts in seats." VPNs (Virtual Private Networks)—the little colored light that informed other workers if you were working on your computer or idle—made it clear that even if you were working from home, you had been away from your desk too long. Companies that treat employees like robots end up with employees who pretend to work. We all know we can sit in a seat staring at a computer and be doing very little actual work. In fact, I get my best ideas when I am at the gym, on a walk with my dogs, or in the shower.

The modern work world requires flexibility, even for companies that are not comfortable offering it. If you want to attract and retain the best people, they are going to demand working conditions that they individually prefer.

I am a believer in remote work. The idea is finally becoming normal, as globally 70 percent of workers work remotely at least once per week.[30] People who work for companies that do not allow remote work are frustrated, with 52 percent saying they wish they could work from home. Companies can save money and retain staff with more flexible work policies, like Dell saving $12 million per year in real estate costs by encouraging employees to work from home. Having to choose between long everyday commutes or expensive housing near the workplace adds to employee stress.[31]

I believe that if you offer your people flexible work environments they will be less stressed out, and they can use that commute time outside of work to take better care of themselves and their families, which is better for your business. Creating environments that are less stressful enables your team to spend more time on the things that matter. More than 90 percent of executives in a Duke study of more than 1,800 CEOs and CFOs said culture is important at their firms. More than half said corporate culture influences productivity, creativity, profitability, firm value, and growth rates. If culture is as important as we say it is, we must be intentional about it.[32]

A company should provide the overarching mission and values of the company, but the way those values come into practice day-to-day is shaped by the manager, and the manager plays an incredible role in shaping company culture. Managers are incredibly important because they impact employees' experience of work. They say people don't leave companies, they leave their bosses. How is your company equipping your managers with the tools they need to do their jobs?

You can create a customer-focused culture, but you shouldn't be destroying your employee's lives in pursuit of customer experience excellence. Eventually word will get out, and this makes your brand look bad. You should be able to have a culture where people feel safe, enjoy contributing, and experience personal growth. You should have customers who enjoy the fruit of those contented employees. Burning through staff is not sustainable, and today, with so much transparency over work experiences from websites like Glassdoor, you can't operate like no one is watching.

My husband, Jacob Morgan, wrote a book called *The Employee Experience Advantage*, in which he describes culture as the side effects of working for your company—which can be good or bad. These side effects are similar to how we think about customer experience. The culture of the organization impacts how employees are treated, the products or services that are created, the partnerships that are established, and how employees get their work done. Regardless of whether the organization is aware of their culture, the culture exists. But since you can't see, touch, taste, or feel it, at times culture is an intangible. Culture gets lost.

One major obstacle to building a positive culture is ego. How do we build an organization where teams are rewarded for supporting one another, rather than competing with their teammates? It makes sense that most people have personal career and growth aspirations, and that is the motivator for their work, but companies must create environments where rugged individualism is not rewarded. Rewards and recognitions programs can make people feel great—but not when employees are clawing each other's eyes out in order to catch the carrot.

If you've had many jobs over the years, then you have worked in a variety of cultures. While the company can intentionally create a particular culture, it is your boss who ultimately sets the tone for your day-to-day worklife.

THE NO-ASSHOLE RULE

Your employee experience is largely shaped by your direct manager and by the people you work with every day. One bad apple on a team can ruin the culture of the entire team. Some of the best companies have a policy of zero tolerance for bullies.

Dr. Robert Sutton was a professor at Stanford University. One of his colleagues proposed that the school hire a renowned researcher from another school. The group was sitting around talking about it and one colleague responded, "Listen, I don't care if that guy won the Nobel Prize . . . I just don't want any assholes ruining our group." The professors laughed about it. But later the group started talking about the idea of the "no-asshole rule" seriously, and they realized that they truly did not want any demeaning or arrogant colleagues. They started to ask a new question before hiring anyone: "Would this hire violate our no-asshole rule?" And this approach worked for Dr. Sutton's department.

It makes sense that how we feel at work greatly impacts the customer experience. If you run a restaurant, and the chef and the sous chef do not get along in the kitchen, their anger or tears will drip into the food.

Many years ago, I worked for a large company. When I started, I was hired by a woman I greatly admired. She was likeable, smart, respected at the company, and someone who got things done. She was a great manager in that she cared deeply about her team, and she called herself a mama bear. Everyone on the team trusted her, and I felt supported at work. I worked remotely and would fly to different locations when they needed me or go to the offices in Silicon Valley.

I will never forget when I got the call from her that things would now change for me at work. I heard a voicemail from her as I deplaned from a work trip. She told me she was being replaced by someone else. I knew I had a special rapport with my prior boss; she had hired me for reasons other bosses might not like, such as social media influence. I knew I was an oddball in the customer service organization where I worked, and she understood me, where I assumed my new boss would not. I had a sense he would not support me, or mentor me as my former boss had done tirelessly. And my foresight was correct. As time went on, it was clear he and I did not have a great working relationship. Eventually it was clear to me he and other managers wanted me out. I became paranoid, especially because the general manager of our division was frequently looking at my LinkedIn profile. I knew they did not like that I was continuing to share my ideas on social media and building my brand, but this scrutiny made me paranoid.

Eventually I was laid off from the company. When I was laid off, my boss could not be at the exit interview. Instead, I was to meet with a manager who was doing my manager a favor by having me sign the paperwork. She sat with me in the lobby of this company for the exit interview and ran our exit interview and meeting while running another meeting on her phone with her laptop out. My exit interview was conducted by someone who was literally multitasking. Ironically, this is a company that is often given awards for being a great place to work. But it's a reminder that an employee's experience of a company can be directly impacted by their boss more than anything.

CREATING A CULTURE CAN BE hard. And creating a customer-focused culture is even more challenging. You are not taking the path of least resistance; you are being intentional about the outcomes you'd like to see no matter how far the distance. Those outcomes require a committed focus on the customer, and that starts with your own employees.

Culture isn't just about feelings, it's about optimizing efficiencies in the workplace so people struggle less. Culture is about creating an environment that is good for the well-being of the entire group, not just one or two people.

An example of a strong culture is Pixar, cofounded by Ed Catmull, author of *Creativity, Inc.: Overcoming the Unseen Forces That Stand in the Way of True Inspiration*. Catmull started from the presumption that employees at Pixar were talented and wanted to contribute. He said he accepted the fact that, even though they don't mean to, the company "stifles that talent in myriad unseen ways." His leadership team would identify those "impediments" and fix them. At Pixar, Catmull felt his job was to create an environment where smart, ambitious people could work with each other effectively. He said, "The way I see it, my job as a manager is to create a fertile environment, keep it healthy, and watch for the things that undermine it."

This approach means assuming you hire amazing people who want to do a good job. It's a humble approach to leadership. The question is, how do we create a fertile environment and what does it take to keep that environment healthy? Modern customers demand an employee who is treated like an adult at work. An "adult" employee is empowered to actually do things for customers. The worst customer experiences are created by environments where adults are treated like children or robots reading scripts. In these cultures, employees may have innovative ideas to improve the company and its products and services, but are told to simply keep their heads down and follow directions.

Today's most admired companies are powered by innovative cultures, where employees are empowered to speak up. These customer-focused cultures are created to optimize employee performance, but also create fertile environments for innovation. In the past, companies were successful because they focused on operational efficiency, putting many people through the same experience. But today's employees and customers want to be treated like individuals. Companies today cannot afford to miss opportunities to innovate, to improve efficiencies. One small improvement in efficiency can mean major success for a business tomorrow.

CAPITAL ONE:
"OVERMANAGE THE THINGS YOU CARE ABOUT"

Capital One manages $373 billion in assets, has almost 50,000 employees, and generates $30 billion in revenue a year.[33] It has a culture with strong ethics, integrity, and a culture of kindness from its beginning thirty-one years ago. The company has continued to embrace change, and gone through transformations in order to become a leading digital bank.[34] What sets Capital One apart and allows this company to grow so quickly?

Magic happens at Capital One, the type of magic you cannot pay for by a PR firm. Stories come out of the Capital One contact center you cannot make up. A Capital One customer named Christina was dumped by her fiancé. She then had her credit card declined when she moved out and had to buy new furniture. She called the Capital One contact center in tears. An agent named Tonya could hear how upset Christina was and knew this was not simply a transaction—this customer needed her faith restored in the world. Tonya gave Christina 4,500 miles to go on vacation and had a bouquet of flowers sent to Christina's ex-fiancé's house for her so he would be jealous.

This story went viral—resulting in millions of people hearing about Capital One and its culture. This is the type of press a company only gets when employees are empowered to do something above and beyond for a customer. Today, thanks to the internet, companies have a new level of transparency: eventually we hear about whatever happens inside your company.

In another story, Mr. Morris, a veteran and Capital One customer, lost a close friend from his days in the Vietnam War. He needed an old picture of a group of friends from their Army days to use at the funeral. He was devastated when he realized he had lost the original photo, and the only remaining version of the photo was printed on his Capital One credit card.

Desperate to get the picture, Mr. Morris called the Capital One contact center and described his situation. The contact center employee didn't know if they could do anything, but after making a few calls and a few exceptions, several departments worked together to get Mr. Morris the photo. They were able to pull the picture from the credit card and even had it framed so Mr. Morris could use it at the funeral.

Everyone reading this book is a customer, and has had the experience of being served by an employee who clearly does not want to be there. We have also been a customer in a situation where we needed more help than the company was willing to provide. The invisible mood-killer for this type of interaction is the company's culture, where employees are not empowered to act on behalf of the customer. While the company might say they care about their employees, their actions speak otherwise. This poor employee experience and toxic culture can destroy the customer experience.

What I have noticed in customer-focused companies is the founder is usually still the CEO, able to make long-term decisions that are good for the business. That is the case with Capital One, which still has founder Richard Fairbank at the helm. Fairbank is famous for only taking a $1 salary for the last twenty years and for blocking his schedule to spend two and a half hours with his family every night.[35] For the last four years, Capital One has made the "Best Companies to Work For" list.[36]

I wanted to find out who was responsible for this powerful culture—a company that clearly embraces the connection between employee experience and customer experience. Through word of mouth I connected with Doug Woodard, an SVP of Customer Operations responsible for 15,000 employees. He told me in a recent phone interview he believes in cultural transparency—when employees are unhappy, customers can feel it. And building a work experience for the people who work directly with your customers matters even more. Woodard believes when it comes to company culture, "companies don't spend enough time thinking about it." He doesn't understand why other companies would not be intentional about their design of a culture. He told me, "We obsess over what it's like to work here."

The Capital One executive team is in agreement that their people are their greatest asset, and they know the culture/employee experience pieces are directly correlated with customer experience. Woodard said, "Between purpose and function, it's easy in our line of work to get wrapped up in function. What's our function? We answer the phone for a credit card company." Woodard believes that "answering phones" is not inspiring. He said, "If you can give people that sense at work—that's when you unleash real potential." He understands it's easy in operations to obsess over service levels and average handle time and staffing. He says he does track many of the metrics that are customary in a call center, but he is more focused on purpose than anything else. Woodard believes in treating his people well and giving them a sense of purpose when they get out of bed in the morning.

The call center is usually seen as a cost center, so riddled with rigid rules and structure that agents sound like robots. Many companies force their call center reps to say the customer's name three times, which can lead to agents awkwardly repeating a customer's name at the very end of the call because they forget to do so earlier.

Woodard's leadership style and worldview make sense when you look at the viral customer experience stories coming out of Capital One. For example, I can imagine when Tonya started her job, she did not know it would entail becoming a guest on *The Ellen Show*.

CULTURE IS OFTEN RELEGATED TO human resources, but this is a missed opportunity because human resources are not in the weeds with their teams every day as managers are. In fact, human resources are feared—they are gatekeepers, the group that keeps the company from being sued. Human resources is not the division you go to when you literally need resources as a human being.

Woodard takes a page from Disney, which believes you should overmanage the things that matter most. Woodard's team has been successful by putting mechanisms in place such as intentional metrics that support the culture they intended to create. These mechanisms build a culture that reinforces their brand and their value proposition. He believes the hard part is drilling down to the actual behaviors you want to drive. For example, Woodard is considering the behavior of his one thousand managers, who each manage a team of fifteen. He believes in being intentional not only about what you measure, but what you don't measure. For example, in customer service at Capital One, there are no sales conversion rates tracked. As a customer, there is nothing worse than when you have a problem and the employee tries to make more money off you. He understands most customers sign up for credit cards online, and this frees employees up to simply focus on the service part of the work.

Contact center metrics like average handle time are tracked, but management only steps in when there are outliers in the call times. The agents have a range; Woodard said, "There are calls that are just a few minutes, but the calls that moved me to tears were longer than half an hour." Money is emotional for people. A person who loses a wallet or has a credit card stolen—that is an opportunity to be there for the customer at the point of need. It's an interaction that the customer won't forget. Employees who do not feel like prisoners of a performance measurement system are going to improve customer experience, and solve the problem faster and more efficiently.

We are human beings and we don't stop being human when we get to work. We are afraid of robots taking our jobs; however, we already treat our employees like robots, and they talk to our customers like robots. Capital One does the opposite of that, and is thriving.

Lessons from Capital One

- ▶ Overinvest and overmanage culture.
- ▶ Be intentional about the culture you design, and start with purpose.
- ▶ Care as much about what you measure as what you don't measure.

Creating a culture that is both employee-focused and customer-focused is not easy. If we want to differentiate our business from the rest, we have to face the reality that the way we manage our internal operations, the way we create experiences for our employees, greatly impacts customer experience.

President Kennedy wanted to put a man on the moon and it was a major focus of his administration. During a tour of the space center in 1962, President Kennedy asked what the janitor was doing, and the janitor looked at President Kennedy and said, "I am helping to put a man on the moon." In a speech on September 12, 1962, Kennedy said about his dream of going to the moon:

> We choose to go to the Moon in this decade and do the other things, not because they are easy, but because they are hard; because that goal will serve to organize and measure

the best of our energies and skills, because that challenge is one that we are willing to accept, one we are unwilling to postpone.[37]

Anyone can open a business, but not everyone can create a customer-focused business as a result of a customer experience mindset and a customer-focused culture. Anyone can hire employees, but not everyone can inspire greatness and a universal vision in every single employee at the company. In the next chapter, we'll learn about customer-focused leadership, and the qualities we need to hire and develop in our leaders.

3

DEVELOPING CUSTOMER-FOCUSED LEADERSHIP

> Your job as leader is to stay as close in touch as possible with those closest to the action.
> —KAT COLE[1]

I used to work at a big company that would say, when there was a problem, "don't look up." This bothered me because I always believed that leadership mattered a great deal. People need leaders. They need transformational leaders able to guide the company in a storm, that can inspire greatness in employees and make powerful decisions or hard calls. My bosses that were great leaders were the ones who most impacted my life and career. It wasn't just the work they requested of me, it was the way they carried themselves, their worldviews, the things they said—it was their reactions to difficult situations. In today's complicated business environment, at a time when trust sometimes feels at an all-time low, the world requires transformational leaders that are self-aware, humble, and build trust. They are proactive, able to make difficult decisions, adaptive, innovative, work independently, and self-manage. Most importantly, they are able to set the vision and motivate employees.

Leadership is one of the most important and overlooked pieces of customer experience, and it should be your starting place for a customer experience transformation.

Customer experience can seem intangible. People think it's something finite they can fix or solve. They want to pin customer experience on one person or one group, and simply be done with it. I remember when I worked in customer service, for a Fortune 500 company, and there was a group they started called customer experience but I was never sure what they did and we never talked. When I asked, I was told they produced events for our top customers.

This is a common story at corporations across the world, where one person or one group is tasked with customer experience. But if you believe that everyone at the company impacts customer experience in some way, throwing a few resources at it won't make the cut.

Why is it that so many companies coach and develop their leaders but they don't coach them to have a customer experience mindset? Leadership development is often simply about developing managers who can create a culture of "followship" within the company. Customer experience requires leaders to fly above the chaos and recognize patterns, opportunities, and efficiencies. In most corporations, managers are promoted and developed for function over purpose. An executive that makes or saves the company a lot of money will be rewarded. This does not mean they will be a great leader.

Leadership development programs must be created with the customer experience mindset. But leaders are generally hired not to bring a customer experience mindset to the company, but to save the company. When business is bad, we become risk-averse. Consultants like corporate downsizer Ryan Bingham (played by George Clooney in the movie *Up in the Air*) are brought in to calculate productivity rates, measure the performance of employees—and make large cuts across the organization.

In start-ups, senior level executives are brought in to make the company more "adult." Executives are often brought in from other successful companies with the hopes that one leader can replicate what they did elsewhere.

Have you noticed that companies that are innovative and customer-focused often are run by founder-CEOs? Charlene Li, Founder and Principal Analyst at Altimeter, brought this to my attention a few years ago when I asked her about which companies do customer experience well.

These executives care deeply about their companies because they literally birthed them. They have the authority on the board to make long-term decisions that are in the best interests of the customer. These leaders do not mind being misunderstood for long periods of time. Examples of founder-CEOs include Amazon, Capital One, Nvidia, Netflix, Apple, Whole Foods Market, Tesla, Slack, Lyft, Spotify, and Airbnb.

In most cases, companies do not have founder-CEOs. But how important is the CEO in a company's ability to be customer experience focused? According to analysts that believe in leadership development, the answer is "not very." Industry analyst Josh Bersin wrote, "While the CEO is a very important person, our research shows that enduring business performance is really driven at much deeper levels: a focus on leadership strategy." This idea that one person can save or completely change a company is simply unrealistic. High-performing companies develop their own unique, research-based leadership model. They don't just hire a consultant or send people to leadership courses.[2] As Bersin states, long-term business performance comes from leadership culture and the careful and continuous development of leadership at all levels. The best companies develop leaders from the bottom up. Senior executives serve the needs of line leaders, like an inverse pyramid.

The company doesn't expect one person to step in and make the company customer-focused. One of the most important things a newly appointed CEO must do is assess the current leadership culture, and then decide how it should change. If the CEO sees too much complacency or lack of alignment, it's up to the CEO to drive a new culture of teamwork and accountability. Only when that message reaches the troops will the company turn around. The CEO willing to empower brilliant and talented leaders in support of the company's leadership culture is the better leader. The CEO must focus on development, but the entire leadership team has to be on board as well.

While I don't believe Amazon has done culture perfectly, the focus on the customer has never veered off course. Amazon's value and mission is not different than it was at Amazon's inception in 1995. The company is consistent, and leaders are developed alongside Jeff Bezos. Bezos keeps a group of talented savants around him, although Bezos famously never hired a COO or president, and didn't ever take the thought of replacing himself seriously. The customer experience mindset is so strong within Amazon that there isn't much waywardness when it comes to developing customer-focused leaders. If you aren't willing to do what is necessary to provide value to the customer, then you're out.

You need to find people with the attributes necessary to fit the customer experience mindset and help develop them so they can be successful in your company. Transformational leaders are not going to stay in companies that are not employee- or customer-focused. You have to hire people who are in tune with your company's value set, and then develop and empower them to be successful.

Your employee base is changing. Many of your employees are millennials or their gen Z siblings. These employees are digital natives who feel comfortable expressing themselves in almost any environment. They have seen the power of cultural movements such as #BlackLivesMatter and #MeToo. Today's environment requires approachable, flexible leaders who are intuitive, who are culturally sensitive and understanding, who are trustworthy.

ADMIRAL VERNON CLARK

Admiral Vernon Clark served from Vietnam through the Gulf War, and received dozens of awards for his leadership and bravery. As Chief of Naval Operations, Clark restored pride in the Navy through his leadership development, and he is known for creating a healthy culture in the Navy.[3] He valued personal growth and continuous improvement, saying, "If you are not growing, in my view you are of little value to the institution . . . if you are not growing, you're dead."

He encouraged "constructive friction," which made it safe for people to disagree and express views that were outside the consensus. As a result, Clark's leaders felt connected with him and the US Navy and they emulated his leadership style, which made the sailors under their command feel more connected. Clark required everyone to have a personal development plan. He changed the performance appraisal system to provide constructive feedback for everyone and added a requirement to leaders' performance appraisals that they help sailors learn and grow.

In group meetings he encouraged participants to speak up: His own approachable conversational style set the tone for others to share their ideas and opinions. He asked everyone to "challenge every assumption," "be data driven," and "drill down" into the details. "Have a sense of urgency to make the Navy better every day."[4]

It can be hard to maintain a customer-focused culture because not only do you have to find amazing people, but you are developing people from all different backgrounds and walks of life. You might need to take an approach and fine-tune it so people who are used to communicating in different ways can align with the effort.

Some of these skills, mindsets, and behaviors you can hire for, but you also need a culture that develops and supports these qualities. Companies that offer a supreme customer experience are more focused than other companies. They do not lose sight of the target. We don't often think about what customer-focused leaders should be, or how to develop them, but we should.

Customer-focused leaders do not work to get themselves promoted, or even to make their own team look good. They are thinking about the entire ship on which they stand. In order to understand the customer-focused leader, I have organized twenty traits into five categories. These categories include the energy for influencing change, the modern neighborly leader, good judgment, can-do attitude, problem-solving, and consistent say-do ratio.

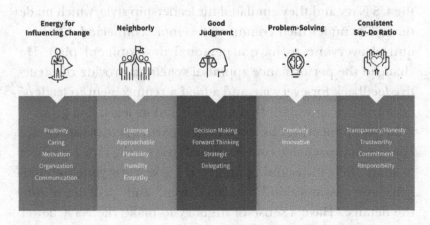

Five Qualities of the Customer Experience Leader

Energy for Influencing Change	Neighborly	Good Judgment	Problem-Solving	Consistent Say-Do Ratio
Positivity	Listening	Decision Making	Creativity	Transparency/Honesty
Caring	Approachable	Forward Thinking	Innovative	Trustworthy
Motivation	Flexibility	Strategic		Commitment
Organization	Humility	Delegating		Responsibility
Communication	Empathy			

THE ENERGY FOR INFLUENCING CHANGE

Great leadership requires hard work. Many of us have met people who simply have great energy. These are confident, genuine people that change the molecules in the room. They aren't necessarily charismatic, but they inspire greatness in others. They are expert communicators, knowing how to verbally frame every situation. These are your customer-focused leaders because they have the energy for influencing change—and they will need it because transformation requires an elevated energy level. Being customer-centric, working hard on behalf of the customer, can take its toll on employees. Those employees benefit from being led by positive, caring, motivating, and organized leaders. You not only need to have the energy to influence change, but you must have the energy to organize it. Most companies today have complicated organizational structures and multiple projects and programs going at one time. Today's leaders must know how to be incredibly organized in order to keep all balls in the air at once. Let's drill down into why customer-focused executives are positive, caring, motivating, and organized.

Positivity. Have you ever known people who seem to accomplish so much, and whistle while they work? In my own life these are people who don't complain much and get more accomplished than those who are fearful and negative. Often our most customer-centric leaders are the most positive leaders—they are not intimidated by challenging circumstances. They see customer problems as a chance to fix what is broken. There is a theory that supports the idea called "broaden-and-build." This research experiment conducted in 1988 shows that being positive sparks the urge to play, explore, be more creative, and inspire big-picture inventiveness. All of these things help leaders succeed at work.[5] Successful people are often extremely positive. Netflix CEO Reed Hastings once said that as Netflix grew from 10 to 640 employees, he was "underwater" and in over his head. He was doing white-water kayaking at the time, and in kayaking if you stare at the problem, you are much more likely to hit danger. He said, "I focused on the safe water and what I wanted to happen. I didn't listen to the skeptics." When stressful situations arise, leaders like Hastings are capable of focusing on the positive outcome rather than what is going wrong.[6]

Caring. I've been in the customer experience space for over ten years, and I have found that the people who work in customer-facing fields are often some of the more caring and empathetic people I've met. Working in customer-facing roles can be hard, and you must be genuine, or customers will not trust you. You don't have to run around pouring your heart out at work, but to be a successful leader you've got to care more. That level of "caring" will make you glow, and that glow will inspire everyone around you. If you don't care, you will not last. If you have trouble caring, try ways to reframe the situation. Think of how you would personally feel if you were in the customer's situation. If the situation involves an employee, imagine what life was like for you when you started out in the business world. Most of us develop some skinned knees and bruises along the way. So have empathy for those who are still developing themselves and learning how to operate in the world.

Motivation. Do you have any friends that make you want to be a better person? Incredible leaders hold themselves to high standards and inspire other people to be better and do better. They are able to motivate themselves and they are able to motivate employees to rise above. There is so much distraction in today's world, leaders who get individuals to operate above the fray are more important than ever. These are leaders who care deeply about individual customers, and feel personally responsible for that customer experience. This is why founder-CEOs care about the experience as much as they do. They care about the product or service they built because it is their baby. How do we bring in external people to lead and make them feel as accountable to the customer as a founder? The answer lies in good people, and putting the right people in the right positions. There isn't always a one-size-fits-all approach, and what motivates employees that work on the factory floor won't work for your engineers, and what works for your engineers won't work for your recruiters or salespeople.

Organization. Today's fast-paced companies have many projects going at once. Most customer-focused companies see themselves as more of a lab than a factory, which means trying a lot of new things. It can be hard to stay organized with so many moving parts. Great leaders must be incredibly organized. You don't need to be a perfectionist, but the best way to combat stress is to make your life more efficient. By being organized, you cut down on waste and you are more pointed in your time and resource management—allowing you to be more calm and more effective in your personal life and at work. An organized leader prevents chaos and makes for happier employees and smoother customer processes.

Communication. We live in a world where connectivity is currency. From mass emails to instant messages to text messages to in-person conversations, leaders know how to communicate clearly and powerfully. Modern leaders also know when to say nothing, or delay a reaction. Anything you say can be misconstrued, or recorded and shared out of context with thousands of people. We must be able to say what we mean, and if that is misunderstood, clear up any misunderstandings. Modern leaders are able to communicate a concise message on the appropriate channel. They understand cultural nuance and subtext. These leaders are out on the floor communicating daily with employees as well as with customers.

NEIGHBORLY

What does it mean to be neighborly? If something went wrong on your street, you would be kind enough to chat with your neighbors about it. When you hear about today's most customer-focused companies, when the senior executives are described—even CEOs—you hear that they are involved in the day-to-day operations. These are leaders who enjoy being in the factories and on the floor with employees. They treat the barista at the corporate cafeteria as well as they treat the board members. Increased transparency, social media, millennial attitudes, shifting gender stereotypes, and more diverse leadership teams have all contributed to the new standard for leadership. This new standard is a more humble, approachable style where leaders actually listen to what employees have to say, and to their ideas for improving the company.

Listening. They say if you want to be a great writer you must be a great reader. The same is true of being a great speaker: You must first be a great listener. I recently met a woman who works with Jeff Bezos at Amazon, and she said of working with him, "He really listens to what you have to say, like you are the only person in the room." Have you noticed that most people don't listen, but often simply wait for their turn to speak? Modern leaders listen to employees and customers, and welcome feedback. They apply what they hear, involve external voices, and consider what would be best for customers.

Approachability. Have you ever had the experience of working with someone who has a big ego? This person doesn't listen when others talk, and has an air of "I'm better than you." An isolated executive who doesn't greet employees or know anyone's name alienates everyone. There are dozens of cautionary tales of companies not heeding the warnings of employees, and paying the price later. Companies that did not listen to employee warnings include Equifax, Wells Fargo, Takata, General Motors, Toyota, BP, Cadbury, Samsung, and many others.[7] These companies had public embarrassments that were harmful to customers, to employees, and to the environment. If executives had been approachable and listened to the warnings of employees, the disasters would not have happened. Feedback is incredibly valuable for those that are approachable enough to warrant it.

Flexibility. In today's world, things change quickly. You know this in your own life—where you have a vision for exactly how something should play out, but the world has another idea in store for you. Today's leaders must be versatile and pivot easily in unforeseen circumstances. The only thing you can count on is that unanticipated events will occur. In fact, poor customer experiences are often a result of overly engineered customer experiences, where customer service agents are stuck with inappropriate scripts or employees across departments do not have autonomy. Leaders must be flexible and able to deal with variation without losing their cool.

Humility. Humility is a big trait when it comes to customer experience because every trait listed here is related to being humble. A humble leader is willing to hear about the ugly truths of an employee or customer experience. Employees will not trust an arrogant leader: leaders must be humble enough to realize that it isn't all about them. They are willing to sacrifice their time, energy, and resources to make sure other people succeed. If someone is humble, they are not simply going to do things because it will give them a promotion, but because it is the right thing to do for an employee or a customer. Today's most popular CEOs are shockingly humble.

Empathy. Some of the most empathetic people have been through very hard stuff in their lives. Being weathered by life's difficulties has made them more empathetic than people who have never struggled. None of us are immune to the pain of being human. We all experience loss, pain, and suffering. These experiences grow us as human beings, giving us a level of empathy for others who experience pain. Empathetic individuals are good at connecting with others because they know pain; they know what it is to struggle. The most customer-focused leaders have a sense of hardship, and as a result they are servant-leaders who are willing to go the extra mile for customers, or put their employees before themselves.

GOOD JUDGMENT

It is true that common sense is not all that common. Customer-focused leaders are able to cut through the noise and make smart, forward-thinking decisions. They don't try and boil the ocean, but delegate to people who are experts. While no one can predict the future, the leader with good judgment can anticipate future needs of customers and the future needs of the business, and can make decisions that consider a balance of those two needs.

Decisionmaking. There's a Latin proverb, "fortune favors the bold." Companies like Amazon have adopted these principles, and they embrace one of their ten leadership strategies, "bias for action."[8] Amazon leaders believe that speed matters in business; if you make a mistake, that decision is likely reversible and shouldn't be hindered by analysis paralysis. Customer experience is enriched by employees who can make on-the-spot decisions for the customer. Terrible customer experiences are fraught with red tape, where employees must wait for a hierarchical decisionmaking process, and everything must be approved by a manager. If you treat your employees like children, they will act like children. Hire good people, develop them, and train them—then get out of the way and let them make decisions. They will work harder for you than employees who are micromanaged. Through life experience you've likely developed an intuition or gut feeling about the right move. Trust yourself, and create a culture where adults are empowered to make decisions without having to get approval from a manager for every instance.

Forward thinking. Being customer-focused means looking at societal behavior change, and seeing how it will impact your business. You are not simply looking at your internal processes, but identifying trends on the horizon. This doesn't mean throwing up a chatbot and thinking you've created a future-ready customer experience. This means looking at the big picture, and at scenarios of what the future could look like. All senior executives have a responsibility to stay up to date on new technologies and changing behavior. Many companies are now hiring futurists to help them identify global trends. Companies that use futurists include car companies like Ford, Google, home improvement big-box stores, global NGOs, the agriculture industry, the hospitality industry, NASA, and the United States Department of Defense/DARPA.[9]

Strategic. Business today is like a chess game. You need to be thinking six moves ahead, and not simply looking at the pieces on the board as they are right now. You can't simply decide you want your company to be customer-focused rather than product-focused. You have to think about resources, timing, and potential roadblocks. While the CEO is responsible for the overarching strategy, the best CEOs leverage their team of experts to look at all possible scenarios; they don't try to come up with a strategy in a vacuum.

Delegating. Great leaders inspire greatness in others, and don't hoard responsibilities or recognition. The best companies today develop leaders who know how to give responsibilities to other people. They do not take credit for the ideas of underlings, but support their people and give them credit when the work is done. This team approach—and delegation—is the way to increase efficiencies—the key to running a smoother business. Today's employees do not like to be micromanaged. Modern software enables more autonomy; however, many companies are not willing to let go and create environments where employees can make decisions for customers or other employees independently of a manager. Poor customer experiences happen when customer-facing employees are not empowered to actually get things done for the customer, and must get approvals from busy and hard-to-reach bosses.

PROBLEM-SOLVING

One thing we know for certain about the future is that life happens. The future does not always unfold as we would like it to. But those who do not panic in times of duress ultimately fare better. In a leadership role, problem-solving must be a focus, particularly when working with customers. Being creative and innovative in how you tackle a problem can translate into huge successes for the company. Those working in customer service know they are in the business of problem-solving, but the entire company is also in the business of solving problems for the customer. Problem-solvers are like great chefs. They take what might seem to be insufficient or uninspired ingredients and create an amazing dish.

Creativity. A creative businessperson is a very good problem-solver. And there is possibly no better example of creativity than Pixar, the beloved producer of movies like *Toy Story, Cars, Coco, WALL-E, Inside Out*, and more. Pixar's rise to success was not a straight climb; it was fraught with complications and near-death experiences for the company. Founder Ed Catmull detailed what makes Pixar so special: "We acknowledge we will always have problems, many of them hidden from our view; that we work hard to uncover these problems, even if doing so means making ourselves uncomfortable; and that, when we come across a problem, we marshal all of our energies to solve it."[10] He said that people could feel this culture and zeitgeist when they would walk into Pixar headquarters, and this creativity was what made the company so successful. Creativity means taking risks, trying to solve a problem using strategies others might not think of.

Innovation. Being innovative is a cousin of being creative. Many of the world's most innovative companies are also the world's most customer-focused companies. The 2018 *Forbes* list of the world's most innovative companies includes Tesla, Netflix, and Amazon.[11] These are companies that value problem-solving, and being creative in solving customer problems. The greatest leaders are like talented artists, applying creative thinking and unorthodox approaches to solve problems. Bold leaders aren't afraid of change: They are hungry to find clever solutions to meet the needs of the business. If you are innovative, then it's likely you are also bold, and you're willing to take big risks to improve the experience of customers. Companies should encourage risk-taking by providing a safety net for employees that fail. If we normalize failure, we will encourage employees to take more risks—which is better for the business in today's competitive environment.

CONSISTENT SAY-DO RATIO

We're facing a trust problem in business. Customers do not trust companies. Employees have a hard time trusting their employers. Creating a culture of trust starts with a strong say-do ratio. This means that executives do what they say they are going to do. Having integrity is a critical trait for modern leaders because a new level of transparency is required for company cultures. Today the world is facing issues such as data privacy and data ethics (see chapter 10), which demand leaders who have integrity and make good decisions for employees and customers.

Honesty and Transparency. Look at any corporation's business page and you will often find a lengthy paragraph about corruption and scandals. From the Enron scandal to Wall Street's crash and the bank bailout to the Facebook Cambridge Analytica privacy breach, people are experiencing corruption fatigue. Both customers and employees demand transparency from the business world and its leaders. As a result of social media, everyone has a voice, and people are making clear they want more honesty from marketing and advertising. From Instagram to YouTube, we are seeing a trend of people and brands getting "real." Despite some misses, the trend toward realness and transparency is not going away. Leaders are expected to be more "real" with employees, and with customers. Being real is valuable, and people trust you more when you make yourself vulnerable. When something goes wrong, it is critical for leaders to be humble and apologize when necessary. With data breaches happening regularly, consumers are growing wary of brands who do not take data privacy seriously. Every day we hear of another company that had a data breach years ago, and only told customers about it once they had to. Leaders need to ensure they are protecting their customers, and when something goes wrong, leaders must immediately communicate about it to the appropriate parties without compromising the company or the customer. Today's world demands transparency.

Trustworthiness. Fostering a culture of trust can be hard given the state of politics, corporate corruption, and the awkward state of culture in a post-#metoo world. How do we foster trust inside the organization? Being trustworthy today is everything. Leaders must not engage in toxic watercooler gossip at work and must stand by their promises to employees and customers.

Commitment. Customer-focused executives have a great sense of responsibility. These executives are committed to the mission of the company and are willing to do what it takes to succeed. Even when times are difficult, they stand by their employees to ensure that the customer promise is delivered on. Amazon is a company that requires deep commitments from its executives. When I went to Amazon, I met a VP of Logistics who goes on 2:00 a.m. ride-alongs with package delivery truck drivers to get a sense of their experience. It is this commitment that has made Amazon so successful.

Responsibility. Being responsible is linked to being humble. Responsible leaders don't blame others when things go wrong or take all the credit when things go right; leaders win and lose with their team. Responsible executives take accountability for failures, are willing to be self-critical, and are focused on improving the process going forward. They are not a just the figurehead in charge of a team, they labor alongside employees to get the work done and make sure it is done right.

BEING A CUSTOMER-FOCUSED LEADER MEANS developing transformational leaders. Customer-focused leadership is leadership that rises above; these leaders go further and work harder than other leaders to ensure their relevance to their own companies, their teams, and their communities. This elite group has incredible integrity, commitment to results—and to their people. These individuals can create a palpable impact at your company, but only if you develop and support them. The best leaders are not born great; they become great over time. Invest in your leaders and they will invest in your employees, who will in turn provide superior experiences to your customers.

4

DESIGNING THE ZERO-FRICTION CUSTOMER EXPERIENCE

> Simplicity is the keynote of all true elegance.
> —COCO CHANEL[1]

Have you felt the powerful shift in the universe between businesses and customers? For decades, companies were able to succeed even when they treated customers badly. But something happened in the last ten years. Riding the coattails of legacy no longer works. Entire industries have been uprooted by unicorns that ride in and simply lift work off of customers' backs. We live in an amazing time, where innovation trumps legacy. A report by Accenture found that, while 93 percent of executives say they know their industry will be disrupted at some point in the next five years, only 20 percent feel they're highly prepared to address the threat of disruption.[2] Companies that will thrive tomorrow are willing to disrupt themselves. They are honest about where their experiences fall short, and willing to address those issues today.

The issue at the heart of a discussion of a zero-friction customer experience is innovation.

In the past when we talked about efficiency, productivity would be discussed as well. Or a conversation about Six Sigma, introduced in 1980 at Motorola, and popularized by Jack Welch at General Electric in 1995. When we talk about creating zero-friction experiences, we have to hat-tip Six Sigma's creators, because their goal was to produce zero defects.[3] When you talk about efficiencies in the past, you might read about W. Edwards Deming, an American engineer, statistician, professor, author, lecturer, and management consultant and the author of *Quality Productivity and Competitive Position*.[4]

Seventy years later and we are no longer talking about productivity, Six Sigma, or quality. But we are still talking about creating efficiencies. Now we have a vastly different world where technology plays an incredible role in our processes and structures. The world is much more complicated than it was when Deming was writing. Quality is table stakes. We can no longer measure success by productivity as we did in the past, such as "butts in seats," or for call center agents, the amount of time a call center agent is on the phone. In today's world, customers do not want to be on the phone with you at all. And many knowledge workers all over the world enjoy remote work thanks to advances in connectivity and changing attitudes toward what is acceptable in company culture. Your next billion-dollar idea could come from an employee who is walking his dog at home on his lunch break. As we shift increasingly toward a technology-powered society, these business principles will continue to fade, as we embrace new management philosophies that are relevant to the new way people live and work today.

Efficiency today is about clear insights into improving the business. Efficiency is innovation, and finding better ways to work. It is about being real. How do our businesses really run? What happens inside our businesses, across the supply chain? Customer experiences also need to be rooted in reality, rather than the assumed way customers are meant to experience products and services. For example, Target CEO Brian Cornell visits customers' homes to understand how they live and shop. Knowing more about customers helps create a more effective customer experience.[5] (You will read more about Target's commitment to the customer in their digital transformation effort in chapter 7.)

Today's leader must be in the weeds as much as they are in the ivory tower. There simply isn't time to let inefficiencies ruin the company. CEOs must always be on the pulse of what both the employee and the customer experience actually are. This knowledge will equip senior leaders with the tools to create more efficiencies—and even small gains on efficiencies can significantly move the needle for customer experience. A survey of more than 1,300 CEOs from around the world found the top thing they plan to do in the next twelve months to drive revenue growth was create operational efficiencies (77 percent).[6]

Some of the worst corporate blunders in the last thirty years happened because senior leaders did not listen to employees who waved a red flag. In business, employees—particularly customer-facing—are often the individuals who have the potential to warn their employers of any problems that might arise.

Efficiency today is baked in empathy. Creating efficiencies means you have walked through both your employee and customer experiences, and you have found ways to make the processes smoother. You understand from a granular level what it's actually like to do the jobs your employees do, or experience the products and services the way your customers do, and make improvements based on firsthand knowledge.

The world has changed, and the power has shifted to the buyer. The customer is happy to leave a legacy company. Companies survive because they make customers' lives easier and better. Companies grow overnight when they figure out more efficient ways to solve common problems. Airbnb has democratized travel, helping customers who were tired of typical hotel stays and wanted other options to stay comfortably and authentically. After nine years, Airbnb had 4 million listings, which is more than the top five major hotel brands combined. Its valuation is $31 billion dollars, more than most major hotel chains.[7]

Many of the most compelling examples of disruption come from finance, where customers demand more seamless ways to manage and exchange their money. Square has changed the lives of small-business owners by creating a convenient device that turns any smartphone into a credit card reader. The company made $3.2 billion in 2018.[8]

Direct-to-consumer companies have been disrupting the market in every sector. They take out the middleman and get customers products directly. For example, shopping for a mattress is difficult, and the mattress industry is inefficient. Casper made it easier for people to buy quality mattresses: They started with a website and later opened showrooms where customers could take naps on the mattresses. Instead of shopping in store and being overwhelmed, the mattresses come straight to customers' doors. Casper became a $100 million company in two years, while traditional mattress companies continue to close retail locations.[9]

The way to avoid disruption today is to be willing to disrupt your own business. Companies must focus on how they can continue to create more seamless and efficient internal processes. In the past, companies have gotten away with veering off the path of being customer-centric. But a customer's tolerance for bad behavior—or poor product performance—is dropping rapidly because customers have ever more choices.

Portrayals of modern life in advertising show photos of attractive, healthy people enjoying a product or service, smiling in wonder at how wonderful life can be. The reality of many products and services is they break. We often create processes that are company-centric, not customer-centric. Customers don't have time for products and services in their lives to break. They don't have extra resources to hand over to a company that is too product-centric, rather than customer-centric. This is why I have created the CX Imperative: the tougher the situation the customer is going through, the more important it is for the company to step up at the point of need.

The CX Imperative

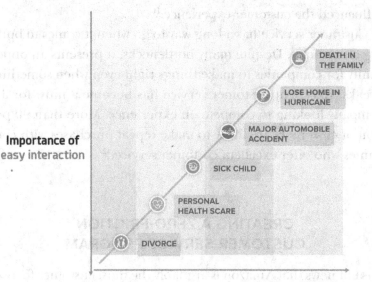

The definition of the word *efficient* is the ability to accomplish something without wasting time, effort, and resources.[10] If you want to focus on customer experience, efficiencies are your first place to start. The role of customer relationship management technology was the process of making companies more efficient, creating records of who the business sold to, and the transaction history of those customers. With advances in technology, we have the ability to do much more than simply keep transactional record histories. For example, the cloud has changed the game for creating efficiencies in customer experience because we can better manage the customer journey and the way we store customer data. The experience cloud is the infrastructure that brings together your audience profiles, CRM (customer relationship management), analytics, content management, commerce, campaign execution, personalization efforts, and engagement efforts to better manage the end-to-end customer experience. Recently a survey was done with a thousand business leaders globally. Almost three-quarters of the companies surveyed said that the cloud has influenced the customer experience.[11]

Customer service has a long way to go when it comes to building efficiencies. Despite many bottlenecks, it presents an opportunity for companies to make things right even when something breaks. Excellent customer service has become a must for any company looking to compete on experience. More than 90 percent of customers are likely to make repeat purchases with companies who offer excellent customer service.[12]

CREATING A ZERO-FRICTION CUSTOMER SERVICE PROGRAM

It is not news that Amazon is arguably the most customer-focused company on earth. We talked about Amazon shaping the customer experience mindset at length in chapter 1. Amazon has gone to the ends of the earth to make everything they do more efficient, and that is how they have successfully scaled their incredible operation. Let's look at how Amazon creates a zero-friction customer service operation in seven acts.

1. Amazon Customer Service

Amazon's customer service team grows every year, as Amazon's business grows in existing geographies and expands to new ones. Amazon has customer service centers in more than thirty-five countries. The Amazon customer service support teams speak seventeen languages, and are available to solve problems at all hours. Additionally, they have a growing team of "virtual" customer service associates, working from home to support customers. These virtual CS roles enable Amazon to accommodate and retain workers with nontraditional schedules. When I was at

Amazon, I met an employee whose husband is in the military and she has been able to move around the world to accommodate her husband. Amazon customer service teams support a variety of customers in addition to those shopping on Amazon's retail websites, such as sellers who offer products on Amazon's marketplaces, as well as authors, advertisers, and drivers who deliver packages for Amazon Logistics.

2. A Global Service Strategy

Amazon aims to solve the customer's problem on every customer contact; this is Amazon customer services' primary measure of success. It's also important that the customer service team responds quickly, and Amazon has the processes and metrics in place to ensure Amazon does that. Amazon has mechanisms in place to look for repeat defects, and then act when they encounter those defects. Measuring all of this and managing it is an important part of how Amazon obsesses over customer experience and creates a zero-friction customer experience.

3. Metrics

Every day, Amazon asks every employee a question. This approach is powerful and helps Amazon understand what's going well and what's not, down to a specific team. The answers are confidential, and only available to a special HR team, but team-level results are shared with managers so that they can make improvements. The daily question could be, "Rate how well your manager listens to your ideas," or "Do you have the tools needed to do your job?" This measurement mechanism has helped to drive countless improvements across Amazon's customer service organization, both for employees and for customers.

4. Leadership Development and Training

Amazon believes everyone at the company is a leader, and they use the Amazon Leadership Principles as a key barometer in hiring, training, and developing their teams. These include characteristics like showing a bias for action, being vocally self-critical, being right a lot, and being customer obsessed. Amazon invests in the ongoing development of leaders, which includes a variety of programs at the site level, and virtual self-development programs as well. Amazon actively works to grow internal talent, and fill open leadership positions with internal talent whenever possible. Newly hired customer service field managers come to the Seattle headquarters for a weeklong development course where they work closely with Amazon's corporate leadership team and go through a sort of masters-level course on customer obsession and leadership. Amazon also has a women's leadership development program in the customer service team.

5. Data Is Part of Everyday Management of Customer Service

Amazon has robust mechanisms for using data in their customer service functions. Amazon also has mechanisms in place to listen to and leverage anecdotal data. Thanks to advancements in machine learning, they're making strides in finding the needles in the haystack, which allow Amazon to quickly detect and solve even small problems such as problems with delivery in a particular zip code, or unusual rates of return on a problem product.

6. Amazon Empowers Their Teams

Amazon believes they succeed when they are able to hire people who share an obsession for customer experience, train them effectively, and then empower them to do the job. They believe it's much better for customers, and therefore the long-term success of the business, versus setting top-down budgets for "variation" or "apology" situations. One interesting mechanism that has proven to be very successful at both defect reduction and successfully engaging Amazon's workforce is the customer service "andon cord." The idea comes from Toyota, whose production system is famous for attention to detail and employee engagement. At a Toyota factory, everyone on the factory floor owns the quality of the product, not just some "QA Team" that checks things at the exit door before a car leaves the factory. If a factory worker discovers a defect coming down the line, they are expected to "stop the line" by literally pulling a cord. This allows the team to immediately go upstream, find where the defect occurred, and fix it at the root cause. When a customer contacts Amazon and they identify it as a repeat defect about a specific product they sell, the CS associate "pulls the andon cord," disabling the product on the website and preventing other customers from buying it. A clock starts, and a process is engaged to inspect inventory in the warehouse, and fix any errors on the website. Only after the root cause is fixed is the product reenabled for purchase. This is an effective mechanism for driving down defects. And it's also a lot more fun at Amazon to be a customer service associate who can actually take action and be part of the improvement process.

7. How Amazon Measures Team Success

Amazon leaders obsess over the metrics and mechanisms they have for managing customer experience, employee engagement, and performance improvement of the organization. They take a balanced approach in how they blend these things together, and customer service leadership inspects them regularly. But the most important thing the customer service team can do is to be an effective voice of the customer, channeling the needs of customers back to the rest of the organization. Measuring and improving how Amazon employees do that is one of the most rewarding things for Amazon executives.

Zero-Friction Customer Service Lessons from Amazon

- Virtual employees can help your company scale quickly, and are a good resource. Hire military spouses and people who have to move frequently and give them the opportunity to work from home.
- Measure closure rate and the speed it takes to close customer service issues.
- Ask your employees a question every day to ensure honesty, transparency, and an understanding of what's happening on the ground with your individual employees.
- Use machine learning to look for outliers and particular defects.
- Empower your employees to make snap judgements to solve customer issues.
- Enable employees to pull the andon cord when they see a defect that could affect many customers.
- Ensure your KPIs measure customer experience, employee engagement, and performance improvement of the organization.

ZERO-FRICTION IN HEALTHCARE

Inefficiency is still rampant in today's customer experience. More than three-quarters of consumers say inefficient customer experiences detract from their quality of life.[13] The last time you went to the doctor, how was that experience for you? Or the last time you went to the grocery store, or the last time you had an issue with your cable, or your insurance. In healthcare a poor customer experience can literally mean death. I would bet that you—reading this book—had some type of miscommunication in a healthcare situation at some point that was dangerous or potentially dangerous. Death due to medical error is a real threat facing the US, with 250,000 deaths per year as a result.[14] There are a few ways to begin to understand how to create more efficiencies in our businesses. We will hear about these ideas again and again in this book, because they are often the tenets of companies that have focused on efficiency from the beginning.

The Latin root for *hospital* is from the Old French *hoste*, which means *host* or *guest*. That's not what we think of when we imagine a hospital today.

Too often we take what is presented without asking why. For example, why can't a hospital be more like a luxury hotel than a hospital? When I think of a hospital, I think of fear and bad vibes. Patients are afraid of staff, and staff are scared of being sued. We think of aloof doctors and underappreciated administration. Vulnerable patients feel like they are stuffed into a system that doesn't want them there. The hospital that morphs itself into a luxury hotel—now that's something to think about. It all comes down to innovation and customer experience. In a recent survey, 92 percent of healthcare consumers said improving customer experience should be a top strategic priority for medical providers over the next twelve months, increasing from 71 percent last year.[15]

Customers today are stuck in stilted experiences without choice. One in eight patients left a practice in the last year, and it's likely the other seven would leave if they had a better option.[16]

But today we're starting to see the consumerization of healthcare. Do we design our hospitals and patient experiences while considering that we are creating an experience for a patient and their loved ones? How do loved ones feel when hospital staff communicate with them? What is it like in the waiting room? Do we make it easy for people to get information they can clearly understand? It is likely that, in the future, we will not even have hospitals as we know them today; large real estate housing hundreds of sick people under one roof. It's more sustainable to focus on tele-medicine and at-home care. If we can focus on remote monitoring, we won't need ninety-year-olds to endanger their lives simply crossing town to get to a hospital.

One Medical is an example of zero-friction customer experiences. They intend to change healthcare. A unicorn that has raised half a billion dollars, they are gaining traction as a partner to the healthcare system. In most healthcare environments, it takes twenty-four days to get an appointment. In many hospitals appointments do not start on time, and patients are stuck waiting. They wait in the waiting room, then they must go into the doctor's office where they continue to wait in nothing but a gown sitting on top of an awkwardly tall observation table. Research shows that because providers are paid by the volume they see, doctors rush through appointments; experience is a casualty of patient throughput. Studies show the more people doctors see, the lower the satisfaction score.[17]

At One Medical, doctors are salaried and not rushed. Doug Sweeny, CMO of One Medical, told me in a Skype interview, "From the beginning, technology was a core part of the offering." He explained, "What if you were actually able to book an appointment in a calendar on your phone?" One Medical has taken the friction out of the healthcare experience. A concierge health service that has revolutionized the patient experience with high-quality care at affordable rates, it offers patients the ability to search for providers through an online portal and make same-day appointments that actually start on time. Everything about One Medical is designed to create an experience that is individualized, from easy online appointment scheduling and text reminders to beautifully designed offices.

Personalized care from providers—including clear communication and sensitivity—is a priority.[18] The offices are painted inviting colors with modern furniture. They serve apple cider in the waiting room. There aren't phones at the front desk, freeing up receptionists to greet patients and talk with them instead of being distracted by phone calls. In contrast to most hospitals, appointments have an average wait time of less than a minute. One Medical has automated much of the paperwork processes to allow healthcare providers to do what they love most—care for patients. Aside from typical healthcare services, One Medical also offers services that patients already seek outside of the hospital, such as mental health coaching, weight management classes, sports medicine, and physical therapy. The purpose is to help members meet their health goals instead of only seeing them when they're sick.

Providers care about their patients and are accessible for follow-up questions after the appointment. As One Medical Group grows, more concierge-style health systems will bloom, and we'll see the healthcare industry continue to evolve in new ways.

Things We Can Learn from One Medical

- Create seamless onboarding so customers can easily sign up for services.
- Automate paperwork where you can; ensure you have walked through the customer journey and that it's easy for the customer.
- Know your employees will work toward the performance goals you put in place, and ensure those metrics are customer-centric.
- When a customer first enters your environment, whether digital or retail, make sure the experience is pleasant.
- Identify the added services you can create around the product to make your offering more attractive to customers.

It's the tedious, minor stuff that creates a great customer experience. Zero-friction customer experiences are created by an obsession with creating operational efficiencies. But it's not just process and operations, it's the people side of your business. As I wrote at the beginning of the book, we are afraid of automation, and that robots will take our jobs and destroy the planet. But we already treat our employees like robots, and they treat our customers like robots. If we can treat our employees like people, they will have more room to go above and beyond for customers when things go wrong—and things always go wrong. Even the most amazing technology breaks, and when it does, is there a person there to fix that experience quickly?

Efficiency is the most unsexy and also underappreciated tool in business. The companies that are able to create an efficiency, however minor, will gain an advantage. Zero-friction customer experiences happen when we look at a process and we believe it can be better, as we learned from Amazon and One Medical. In the next chapter you will learn about how we create efficiencies for the customer by being ready for the future of marketing.

5

CUSTOMER-FOCUSED MARKETING

> What would your marketing look like if your cus-
> tomers signed your paycheck?
> —ANN HANDLEY[1]

The greatest threat to brands today is the future. We cannot know the future, we can only anticipate possible scenarios, and that is what a "futurist" does. We can look at trends and imagine what the future will hold, but we cannot see the future. This is a challenging proposition for brands that try and manage risk while innovating—at a time when their survival depends on it. Companies must look to their CMO to help drive the vision of creating a customer-focused company. The CMO has a critical role in making the company relevant in the lives of consumers tomorrow.

Through my many interviews with CMOs I've discovered that if you thought your CMO needed to be a sociologist in the past, in the future your CMO needs to be the Sherlock Holmes of the C-suite—an intuitive, customer-focused leader. You cannot lose sight of your customers for even one second or your business risks irrelevance. The CMO is in charge of nurturing and maintaining this relationship with your customer.

Sociographics are the characteristics that influence the way people receive and perceive your brand's messages—they define how your market behaves socially. As generation Z becomes the major buyers, these behaviors will matter even more, as they are more particular about the media and content they consume, and the brands they like or trust. Gen Z is already on track to become the largest generation of consumers by the year 2020, and they account for up to $143 billion in direct spending.[2]

Sociology (the study of human behavior) and sociographics (knowing your customer's attitudes, values, influences, hobbies, passions) will both be important to the future CMO.

Is the CMO of the future a CMO at all, or more of a futurist? The CMO has a role in preparing the company for different scenarios that the future may bring. Customer experience, often owned by the CMO, will gain mounting importance in a world where products are commoditized.

CMO of the Future

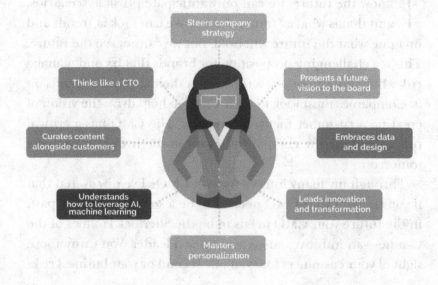

STEERS COMPANY STRATEGY

The CMO of the future must steer company strategy because profits follow companies that obsess over customer behavior. The modern CMO is at the table with the CEO, helping make strategy decisions about the future direction of the company.

A recent study by the CMO Council and Deloitte found that, over the past decade, CMOs have been increasingly asked to elevate their activities from brand and marketing plan management to acting as an enterprise-wide revenue driver.[3]

PRESENTS A FUTURE VISION TO THE BOARD

The mercurial customer of the future will have a great influence on the direction of the company. If the company leaves the CMO out of board-level conversations, the company doesn't understand the importance of the marketing category for the customer of the future. It is critical for the board to hear from the C-level executive that is most connected to the customer. Today the CMO is largely responsible for generating awareness of the company's products and services. The future demands a CMO that is the eyes and ears of the customer and can share these findings with the board. The future brings a CMO that is less focused on simply being in service to sales—and more focused on strategy and overall customer engagement, from company strategy across awareness, education, customer engagement, and service. Three-quarters of marketers said they will be responsible for the end-to-end experience over the customer's lifetime.[4]

IS A DATA AND DESIGN EXTRAORDINAIRE

As we improve the tools to extract insights from our data, CMOs will be held to different standards. Nearly two-thirds of marketing leaders said use of online customer data at their firms increased in the last two years, and 70 percent said they expect to use more online data in the next two years.[5] In the future, customer engagement will balloon in importance and it will be up to the CMO to define what that looks like. As it becomes easier to gather structured and unstructured customer feedback, marketers will be tasked with improving the design of products and services within the company, participating in this customer feedback loop. Studies show only 52 percent of marketers adapt their marketing strategy and tactics based on customer interactions and feedback.[6]

LEADS INNOVATION AND TRANSFORMATION

A customer-focused digital transformation is the redesign of a company organized around the customer. Some companies will hire a Chief Customer Officer or Chief Experience Officer but in my experience that person is often a figurehead with no real influence across divisions or budgetary authority. According to the most recent CCO study, less than a quarter of Fortune 100 companies had a C-level Customer Officer, and only 10 percent of Fortune 500 companies and 6.7 percent of the Fortune 1000 companies.[7]

Today the strongest brands are curating the brand—and its content—alongside its customers. The CMO is the most involved in customer strategy, and increasingly owns all customer programs. It's the CMO's responsibility to know how and when to use new technologies: the CMO is in charge of steering digital transformations. They have to have a seat at the table with the CTO and the CIO in making technology decisions.

A MASTER OF PERSONALIZATION

Personalization reduces acquisition costs as much as 50 percent, lifts revenues by 5 to 15 percent, and increases the efficiency of marketing spend by 10 to 30 percent.[8] In some areas of our lives, we get rich, personalized experiences such as from Amazon, Netflix, Spotify, and Apple products. In other areas, companies have no idea who we are. One study shows 80 percent of customers say they are more likely to do business with a company that personalized experiences, and 90 percent say they find personalization appealing.[9]

Today's personalization amounts to cookies that track you online and an assault of ads that follow you wherever you go. I recently donated to an animal shelter, and since then a similar organization has targeted me for months with pictures of sad-looking dogs out in the cold. While I am happy to give money to a cause I care about, that does not mean I want to see sad-looking dogs all day as I work. Personalization can be a delicate balance between welcome and unwelcome, helpful and creepy, invited and uninvited. The CMO is in charge of knowing the customer and these subtleties.

AI AND MACHINE LEARNING

There has been an explosion of the use of artificial intelligence and machine learning. The share of jobs requiring AI (artificial intelligence) has increased by 450 percent since 2013.[10] Data and analytics are an increasingly big part of marketing. The majority of marketers expect AI to have a greater impact on the way they do their jobs than social media.[11]

CURATES CONTENT ALONGSIDE CUSTOMERS

Customers are more influenced by their peers than they are marketers. User-generated content-based ads get four times higher click-through rates.[12] As many as 90 percent of shoppers report that user-generated content (UGC) influences their purchase decisions.[13] How are you getting to know your customers, highlighting how they are using your products and services, and featuring those stories in your content? One example is cult-brand GoPro, which connects by encouraging customers to upload their best and most inspirational photos and videos to Instagram and YouTube using the dedicated #GoPro hashtag. GoPro also reposts a "Photo of the Day" to Instagram to recognize high-quality photos submitted from brand advocates.[14]

Another example of user-generated content comes from Starbucks, which encourages customers to decorate their coffee cups and upload the pictures with #whitecupcontest. Starbucks shares the best photos on its social media channels.

Airbnb does a beautiful job curating social media, tapping into its inspiring customer stories on its social media and video ads. It highlights places to stay and tells the stories behind Airbnb guests and hosts.[15]

THINKS LIKE A CTO

IT and the technology office must work closely with the CMO to think about digital transformation, and create a technology strategy that is customer- and employee-focused. Nearly three-quarters of marketers have marketing technology management responsibility (also called "martech"). Marketing takes the lead across all martech activities, but collaboration with IT is common.

The CMO has a responsibility to understand the new digital landscape, the technology landscape, and how these technologies can create frictionless experiences for the customer. Since the customer experience starts with the employee experience, we must think about the technology employees have at work, and if employees have zero-friction experiences at work.

FUTURE FOCUS WITH JENNY ROONEY OF *FORBES*

The modern customer is consuming content in a different manner than before. This customer shops in a new way, moving across digital platforms quickly, demanding much. Five years ago, the average consumer typically used two touchpoints when buying an item. Only 7 percent regularly used more than four. Today consumers use an average of almost six touchpoints, with 50 percent regularly using more than four.[16]

Jenny Rooney—longtime editor of the *Forbes* CMO Network—spends her time researching and talking with CMOs. I got to witness this at the Consumer Electronics Show this year where she moderated a panel on a "Future Focus" with *Forbes*'s most influential CMOs. I have been writing for the CMO Network for a few years now covering the intersection between marketing and customer experience. We know that there has been a tsunami of changes in behavior for consuming digital content: the way we consume news, movies, and TV, talk to one another through 1:1 apps, even call our friends and family all over the world using apps like WhatsApp. Marketers have had to learn new ways of maintaining relevance to a customer who has more choices than ever.

According to Rooney, "Now marketers have to think about how that consumer is perusing content. A consumer checking into their phone multiple times a day—they are only patient enough for a few seconds, before the window of opportunity to engage with them is completely closed. That window comes down to seconds in a mobile-first world." The modern customer is looking for snackable content. Rooney says CMOs must create media plans where customers want to engage with a brand immediately and powerfully. "It's a tall order if you look at consumers through the lens of the media consumption habits," said Rooney. CMOs must be on top of their game when it comes to knowing the media consumption habits of their customers, and finding a way to be relevant in their lives.

Today, companies are thinking about their identity—and recognizing that every company today needs to be a data and technology company. In the past we've seen brands, during times of uncertainty, make cuts to marketing, or take away some of the CMO's power and influence. Your CMO should be just as important as your other C-level officers. Today, markets are moving faster than ever. For example, a telecom provider is now an entertainment company (AT&T owns Time Warner). A retailer is now a digital fitness brand (Under Armour owns MyFitnessPal). CVS started as a corner store and is now CVS Health, a broad-based healthcare company after buying Aetna insurance.[17] In the first three quarters of 2018, companies around the world announced merger and acquisition deals worth a total of $3.3 trillion, the most since recordkeeping began nearly four decades ago.[18]

As the market shifts, so do our corporate leaders: Today's CMO needs to be the most customer-focused of the C-level officers, able to watch trends in media, content, and overall branding while other officers have their heads down in the company's products and services. Growth is now part of the CMO's job: identifying major trends, looking at the landscape, and pointing out opportunities for growth. In fact, Coca-Cola has transformed the CMO role into a Chief Growth Officer to reach new consumers and boost brand loyalty.[19]

THE MODERN CMO IS NEVER SILOED

Every year, Rooney compiles a list called "CMO Next" created through qualitative research tapping into the expertise of industry watchers as well as *Forbes*'s editorial industry knowledge. The list features fifty CMOs who are driving brand and business growth.[20] CMOs from the National Hockey League, Converse, Hulu, SoFi, Away, Wayfair, Tinder, National Geographic Partners, Northwestern Mutual, Old Navy, and Cirque de Soleil have all been featured on the list. A common feature of these high-performing marketing leaders is their extensive experience in digital innovation and a focus on building customer relationships with a very human style. Most recently her list featured many CMOs from direct-to-consumer companies that were creating customer-focused marketing programs. That customer-focused CMO has a seat at the table just as much as any other C-level executive. Rooney sees modern CMOs improving the reputation of marketing as a discipline—where customers want to engage with marketing, contribute to marketing, and have a hand in shaping it. Marketers have a great opportunity to be an advocate for the customer relationship inside the company.

More than 40 percent of organizations report that marketing has primary responsibility for customer experience.[21] Rooney believes the art and science of the CMO role has gotten more intense. She said, "There's a lot of pressure and it's a unique role in the C-suite. You have to have a creative mind—an intuitive sense—but you have to have the grounding of data, analytics, and technology."

The future of marketing will see an evolution of the practice—Rooney believes that the organizational structure and processes will change and marketing resources will be organized differently to deliver against the new reality of meeting customers wherever they are. The restructuring of the organization is a necessary part of digital transformation, where marketing is localized, and fluid throughout the company. In the past, organizations were set up vertically, as separate groups—even within marketing there are often many silos, organized by "department" or even "channel." But customers shop horizontally, and they are experiencing too much friction across the different environments.

Customers expect a fluid, horizontal experience, where one experience blends beautifully into the next with no friction or extra effort, according to Jamie Gutfreund, newly appointed Chief Consumer Experience Officer for Hasbro and former Global CMO of advertising firm Wunderman, in a phone interview. The customer expects a horizontal shopping experience from the app to the website to the retail store, but instead she gets an experience full of stops and starts.

Customer experiences are shaped by the employee experience. When a company is organized by channel, that's a problem. If the company is not sharing data across the organization, and collaborating around the customer experience, that's a problem. Customers get varying messages from marketing versus customer service. Customers have to repeat themselves at every turn. Before we lean on technology to assist, we need to have the right organizational structure for success. Once we do get the technology to play with experiential marketing, to use artificial intelligence, machine learning, virtual reality, and augmented reality we can then provide these experiences to customers, CMOs will need to focus on upskilling their employees so employees have the skills to keep up. Hiring will change as companies look to how marketing will play out in a less-siloed, more digital, technology-driven, and automated marketing practice, says Rooney. Today, every employee is a brand marketer, which has big implications for your hiring practices. Who do you want representing your brand? According to Rooney, every employee represents the brand, even if they don't live in the marketing organization.

CAUSE MARKETING AND THE FUTURE CUSTOMER

Generation Z is more concerned about the environment than any other generation. Gen Z is the generation most likely to believe that companies should address urgent social and environmental issues: 94 percent of those surveyed said so (compared to

87 percent of millennials).[22] According to the 2019 Edelman Trust barometer, employer trust is at an all-time high. Globally, "my employer" (75 percent) is significantly more trusted than NGOs (57 percent), business (56 percent), government (48 percent), and media (47 percent). This lack of trust in local governments has employees looking toward their employer to make positive change in the world. In fact, more than three-quarters (76 percent) say they want CEOs to take the lead on change instead of waiting for government to impose it.[23] People are anxious about the future, and they want to work for companies with a conscience. This is a time for CMOs to be mindful and have a point of view. The company must exist for a reason other than simply pushing products; the company must have a moral backbone and a purpose, says Rooney. We are seeing more risk-taking with marketing and advertising—however, marketers do need to be careful they don't alienate or insult their consumer.

THE ROLE OF TECHNOLOGY FOR MARKETING

Marketing has focused for too long on attempting to satisfy the needs of a group of customers rather than individual customers. And often this effort fails. Today technology has given marketers the ability to be more exacting in their approach. In the past marketers would focus on segmentation by looking at attributes such as gender, birthday, and location; however, today marketers have access to structured and unstructured data, which allows them to understand much more about individual customers. Segmenting a customer base is no longer enough. For true accuracy we must lean on technology to get to know the individual customer. Thanks to advances in technology, marketers have many more tools in their arsenal to be able to be more accurate, and drive customer experience. Personalization— shaping an experience for a customer based on individualized preferences—is the future of marketing. Some first movers are already there, such as

Spotify, Netflix, Amazon, and subscription box companies like Ipsy, Dollar Shave Club, Trunk Club, and Stitch Fix. Personalization can reduce acquisition costs by as much as 50 percent, lift revenues by 5 to 15 percent, and increase the efficiency of marketing spend by 10 to 30 percent.[24]

Some of the world's leading brands today are using artificial intelligence and machine learning to know the customer through thousands of data points. This provides marketers with efficiency and accuracy that we have not seen before. And customers crave that personalized experience: just 22 percent of shoppers are satisfied with the level of personalization they currently receive.[25]

Some companies are experimenting with AI, such as Harley-Davidson New York, which increased dealership leads by 2,930 percent in three months. Half of the leads were from look-alikes, prospects with similar buying patterns and preferences as those likely to purchase Harley-Davidsons. This insight opened up an entirely new audience that they had previously not marketed to. The AI uses algorithms to calculate which customers are most likely to purchase and to create targeted messaging toward those customers. It also tracks which digital campaigns are effective and learns as it goes.[26]

Airbnb uses AI to narrow down search results to exactly what each customer will want. The algorithm measures more than a hundred signals at once to personalize searches in real time. Customers are matched with neighborhoods, experiences, and hosts that match their preferences. With AI, click-through rates have increased 21 percent and booking percentages increased 5 percent.[27]

Doesn't it feel good when you spend money with an online retailer, and when you go back to the website or app later you see recommendations that are aligned with who you are as a person? Or even better, you stop by the retail version of this website and they know what you bought in the past and what would nicely supplement your past purchases. But often we walk into a store and the staff have no idea who we are or what we bought in the past.

SPOTIFY

Does anyone talk about their teenage years as the time they felt they had the keys to happiness and in charge of their destiny? I don't think so. The teenage years can be tough ones as children navigate adolescence, and the desire for freedom and autonomy while still living under your parents' roof. The emotions we feel as teenagers are incredibly strong. Perhaps that is why the music we listened to when we were teenagers is the most memorable music of our lives. When a song from our teenage years plays, we are catapulted back to a time of heartbreaks, of seeking freedom from our parents, and of being misunderstood. Enter Spotify, a $5 billion a year music streaming platform with three thousand employees and almost 200 million users. The company started twelve years ago and went public in 2018.

Spotify knows all about your tortured teenage years, and that is why Spotify offers listeners a "Your Time Capsule" playlist full of songs from the Spotify member's youth. Spotify uses a few pieces of information to create this personalized trip down memory lane including your birthday. Your age and your listening history tells Spotify your tastes and preferences. As a result of artificial intelligence and machine learning, the more you listen to music on Spotify, the more the software gets to know you and provide music you like.[28] Spotify is a very data-focused company. They collect twenty thousand pieces of data on each customer. Every time the customer touches the app, Spotify is tracking that behavior. They know if you are walking or running. And they have thousands of pieces of data based on the music you listen to and the playlists you create.

As a customer of Spotify, I'm amazed by how seldom I need to manually change a song, and how accurately Spotify predicts songs that I enjoy. Whether I'm working at my desk or exercising or streaming podcasts for a flight I have to take, Spotify is there with me.

In July 2015, Spotify launched Discover Weekly, two hours of custom-made playlists that are released every Monday mixing a user's personal tastes with songs enjoyed by similar listeners. Customers have listened to billions of tracks. Since this launch, Spotify has launched equally powerful personalized playlists. What does this have to do with marketing? Spotify has used artificial intelligence and machine learning to alter the experience of the user in real time, something marketers can learn from. But only 23 percent of companies are able to integrate customer insights in real time.[29]

Yogesh Chavda, Spotify's former Global Head of Free User Marketing, was responsible for something called "always-on" marketing. Chavda comes from consumer packaged goods, having spent time at Procter & Gamble, Amway, and Kimberly-Clark in various marketing and consumer-insights roles. When he came to Spotify, he had three challenges. First he was tasked with driving consumer acquisition. Second, he needed to increase engagement and retention on the free platform for customers who were not upgrading to the paid service. Third, he needed to reduce churn for users who would abruptly stop using the service.

The first step for Chavda's team was to find out what was really happening with the free users of Spotify. They plotted out every user from the day the app was downloaded through the first year of using the service. They noticed a few things. Some free users upgraded to premium. Other users signed in, then disappeared for a few weeks, then became frequent users of the service. Others signed up and right away were very engaged. Spotify had a lot of variation in the behavior of free users. Chavda engaged his marketing team with the data science team and set out to define what engagement meant to them. Spotify wanted to ensure that the metrics collected by the app correlated with engagement or retention. Chavda's team eventually focused on twelve metrics, including after sign-up what the user was doing in the first two weeks, the first month, and subsequent "inflection points."

They talked to consumers about what issues they were facing from a messaging and playlist perspective. They conducted data science on 26 million users over a twelve-month period, and talked to around a thousand consumers to understand the barriers to retention, reasons for churning, drivers of engagement, and more. They conducted tests to see what was resonating. Once they built a model and framework, they looked at customers in six other countries. This fed into the playlist strategy: Chavda's team finally knew which playlists would drive engagement. From there, Spotify launched more playlists, including personalized user playlists like summer rewind, time capsule, and year in music. These playlists drove a 30 percent increase in subscriptions for free and premium users.

At Spotify, marketing plays an integral role to shape the experience in partnership with R&D (research and development) and the tech community. This is precisely the role of the modern marketer. Spotify manages the complexity of this large operation that includes 22,000 new releases every week. Not only is Spotify using artificial intelligence and machine learning to personalize the music, but machine learning is used to make advertisers happy through targeted placement of advertisements for free users.

Lessons from Spotify

- ► For marketers, personalization leads to engagement and engagement leads to sales.
- ► Collaborate with your data science team.
- ► Use a mix of data science and actually talking to customers to get your marketing approach right.

RUNNING WITHOUT GAS AND RUNNING WITHOUT MARKETING: TESLA

The future of marketing could be no marketing at all. Case in point is Tesla. Much more than a car company, Tesla is a vision for the future, an aspirational brand, a club people want to be a part of. Tesla represents luxury, reducing your carbon footprint, and technological sophistication. People want to buy from Tesla for its ideals as much as for its product.[30]

In 2006, Elon Musk published a blog focused on his "secret master plan" for Tesla. He was aware he could not simply have a goal of mass-producing an all-electric car. He knew design was a critical piece of the equation. He sought to create "an electric car without compromises." His first car, the Roadster, was designed to beat a gasoline sports car like a Porsche or Ferrari in a head-to-head showdown. Recently the Tesla P100D model proved it was the fastest production vehicle in the world.

Consumers care about the aesthetic of the car as much as they care that it is an environmentally good decision to drive electric. The price point of early Teslas made the company enough to be able to continue to create the elevated customer experience that was required. The choice was not to go cheap but to charge more and provide an elegant driving experience.[31]

Many initially made fun of Tesla because of production challenges, not taking the company seriously as it moved from producing zero cars to producing eighty thousand cars per quarter. Tesla is now outselling Porsche, Mercedes-Benz, and BMW, making it the bestselling domestic car in America. In 2018, Tesla stunned the world by showing it could be profitable.[32] This invention finally made a palpable dent on the auto industry. A car run on software, the Tesla can be updated via the cloud, saving frequent service visits. It is cheaper and safer to run than its internal combustion–powered competition.

Its leader brings out passion in people. One CEO of a Fortune 100 company told me privately that Musk gives CEOs a bad name. However, he certainly does inspire evangelism for the products he creates. Few CEOs have become the face of a brand in the same way that Elon Musk has. Musk is CEO of Tesla, and founder of PayPal (which he sold to eBay). He is also the CEO of SolarCity (solar energy services), SpaceX (creating a place for people to live on Mars one day), and The Boring Company (digging tunnels and infrastructure such as Hyperloop).

He is known for sending out tweets asking Tesla customers for feedback; if you read interviews with him, he personally is idealistic and service-oriented. He told *Rolling Stone*, "I try to do useful things. . . . . That's a nice aspiration. And useful means it is of value to the rest of society. Are they useful things that work and make people's lives better, make the future seem better, and actually are better, too? I think we should try to make the future better."[33] While some dismiss Musk, the truth is you can't separate his personal brand from Tesla's.

Recently in the *Consumer Reports* yearly Owner Satisfaction Survey, Tesla finished first, with a whopping 91 percent of owners saying they'd buy a Tesla vehicle if they had to do it all over again. Tesla is a technology-first company that's more inspired by Silicon Valley than its peers in auto. The shopping experience is not what you would find in traditional auto. You do not go to a dealership or haggle with a car salesman. You buy the car online where you can choose the features and customize everything without going anywhere. There are more than 200 stores or galleries in the world, 120 outside of the US.

People care about the aspirations of Tesla, and they share the values of the company. In 2018, Inside EVs estimated that Tesla sold just under 140,000 Model 3s in the US.[34] Tesla has evangelized a community, not simply created a product. The entire auto industry has now followed suit with heavy investments in electric vehicles.

Tesla customers care about the impact they have on the world. Driving a Tesla can be a superior driving experience and technology experience that also reduces the customer's carbon footprint. The entire experience feels modern, personalized, and easier than you would find in a traditional dealership. I interviewed a service manager who runs a team of thirty-two people. (He preferred to remain anonymous.) He said over the phone that customers are into the Tesla mission and "they want to see Tesla succeed." Customers can be demanding at times, but they never threaten to go to another car brand. He said, "If customers see flaws and things they think should be fixed, they tell us because they want us to win." He describes it as tough love, where customers feel part of Tesla's mission. Tesla customers are so happy to refer other customers to a Tesla car that Tesla had to cancel its customer referral program because it became too costly.[35]

OMRON: B2B ROBOTICS COMPANY

When I attended CES this year (the world's largest Consumer Electronics Show with 180,000 people), I was there to look at the robotics floor. If you've ever attended CES then you know it is an ocean of people, events, and things to do and see. But I was there to check out the booth of a new client called Omron, a B2B technology and automation company.

Omron is a Japanese company that was started in 1933. They are known for their medical equipment and for developing the world's first electronic ticket gate (known as a turnstile) as well as being one of the first manufacturers of automated teller machines with magnetic stripe card readers.[36] But in recent years they have generated success in the area of industrial automation, automotive electronics, and "social systems"—the technology you would find in road systems such as traffic lights. They also created the world's first ping-pong playing robot, named Forpheus. And on this cold Las Vegas day I had a ping-pong match ahead of me, versus the robot.

At CES, Omron had exhibited an array of their robots, most of which you would find on a manufacturing floor—robots that move products on an assembly line and assist humans in the creation and distribution of products. But of all the content I posted online about CES, the video montage of me playing ping-pong with the robot generated the most attention. What was fascinating to me was the intuitive power of Forpheus, the ping-pong robot, because he was not just my opponent, he was my coach. In the beginning of our rally, I hit slowly, getting warmed up, trying to focus on getting the ball back over the net without too much force or too little force. As I got more comfortable, the robot's balls came back to me faster. The robot changed its behavior as my behavior changed. At the end of our session, the robot had advice for me on how to hit the ball with better form.

Matt Trowbridge, VP of Marketing at Omron, was hired from GE for his Six Sigma background. One can imagine that marketing robots but also educating customers on them is a big job. Trowbridge said on educating customers, "It's a constant effort. No matter how fast we want to go, if our customers aren't willing or able to run at a similar speed, the results can be disappointing." Omron is constantly offering workshops, webinars, and advisory councils with customers and channel partners. Through this effort, Omron fosters education, ideas, and actions that allow Omron to take the next steps that drive the biggest impact for all involved.

Marketing is the glue that connects the organization, and that glue is stronger with the customer in mind. Marketing leads customer experience at Omron. Trowbridge said all other functions such as sales, operations, and finance have specific tasks they're trying to complete, but the marketing department is the one department that can imagine, create, and intertwine itself with all other internal departments. Additionally, marketing is responsible for communicating customer and market needs. He says, "Marketing's job is to make it easier for everyone else to succeed at what they do, including our customers. It's a big job! It's also the most fun."

Educating customers about new technologies and how to make the most out of them is a critical piece of marketing. But internally, marketing can serve every other department by connecting everyone. At Omron, the marketing department wasn't always customer-focused: Trowbridge went to the CEO and executive team and convinced them Omron needed to become easier to do business with. Not just by improving daily tactical things like placing orders and scheduling service. Omron needed to create their own brand of customer experience based in a digital platform, that contained AI, communicated proactively, and delivered a world-class experience for both customers and employees. Trowbridge said, "We need to be the company we think we are, not who we've been. That's marketing's job!"

Lessons Learned from Omron

- ▶ Educate customers and support them in their growth.
- ▶ Marketing can be the customer-focused glue that connects the different parts of the organization.
- ▶ Marketing can lead the digital platforms that connect the organization.

MARKETING'S ROLE AT ACCORHOTELS

The hospitality industry is changing quickly. The sharing economy has democratized hospitality, making it more competitive for hotels to generate and retain customers. AccorHotels is the largest hotel chain outside the United States, with 4,200 hotels and 250,000 employees worldwide. Before they were my client, I celebrated my wedding partly at The Claremont, their iconic property in Berkeley, California (owned by their Fairmont Hotels brand). Additionally, Accor owns luxury brands Sofitel, Mövenpick, Raffles, European budget brands like Ibis Budget, and midscale brands like Mecure Hotels. These are incredibly varying brands—it is Sharon Cohen's job, as VP of the Fairmont Brand, to build the customer experience from a marketing perspective.

Cohen told me in a phone interview the company is interested in conveying how Fairmont helps contribute to making a traveler's stay both meaningful and memorable—especially the possibility of experiential moments and transformational experiences.

In a world where there are simply too many offerings of the same product and service, how does a company use marketing to stand out? The answer for AccorHotels is reaching out to guests individually and conveying what is most important to them on a personal level. Customers today will pay more for an elevated customer experience, and the Fairmont Brand is looking at what engages guests, like "intimate moments, of memories being made, of minds being opened or perspectives being changed."

This approach requires looking at the design of everything. Cohen still leans on traditional marketing, but is constantly thinking of ways to look at emerging technologies such as voice technology and virtual reality to create a personal and inviting customer experience. The company is highly data-driven and research-focused; Cohen describes the culture as highly collaborative. She said, "Before we develop and execute any marketing initiative, the first thing we want to know is: What are our guests telling us and what are their needs that have yet to be articulated?" Accor is not simply looking at traditional marketing but exploring perspectives of the broader consumer and wider hotel industry. Today, large brands can tap into the power of smaller authentic brands, or even start-ups as Accor has done to continue to evolve. According to Cohen, "One of the many reasons AccorHotels chose to acquire Fairmont Hotels & Resorts was because Fairmont brought a high degree of understanding and level of excellence in the luxury hospitality sector, along with a well-established reputation and scale as a beloved brand in North America and several key markets globally." In return, she said that "Accor's strengths include the global reach, practical and efficient shared services in non-customer-facing areas, and access to procurement power, innovation, creativity, and technological advancements that Fairmont now leverages."

Because companies have so much data today, there may be less emphasis put on the creative aspects of marketing. Cohen describes her approach to marketing as "the creative execution of how we bring our brand to life (art), the expertise we have as leaders in the luxury hotel space operating for over a hundred years (craft), and the data we use to inform all our underlying strategies (science)." She uses data to test how a new idea will be received, even if the entire team feels strongly about it. She said, "It's truly a synergy of data and expertise in constant collaboration that makes us successful: Sacrificing one for the other would be detrimental to our success."

While AccorHotels is a global brand, Cohen travels frequently all over the world to ensure they have "the right product in the right markets." She attributes some of the success of the marketing team to a lot of collaboration and frontline exposure. She visits hotels frequently to see Accor's strategies in action, to witness the guest and employee experience firsthand, and to interpret the way the brand is evolving. Additionally, the entire team gets together twice a year to evaluate progress against annual plans, consult with research teams, and invite discussion from external thought leaders. This might seem trivial, with so much technology to use internally, but how frequently does your own marketing team get together or even meet with stakeholders across the company?

Marketing Lessons Learned from AccorHotels

- ▶ Marketing is still a mix of art, craft, and science.
- ▶ Physically going to see the product or service in action, and understanding it, still matters deeply.
- ▶ Big brands can lean on the authenticity and innovation of smaller brands.

In this chapter you've learned about the CMO of the future and how consumers today demand personalized experiences. In the next chapter we'll expand on the technology side of customer experience, and continue to look at marketing trends throughout the rest of the book as they apply to technology, personalization, analytics, and data ethics.

6

CUSTOMER EXPERIENCE TECHNOLOGY

> The Enlightenment started with essentially philo-
> sophical insights spread by a new technology. Our
> period is moving in the opposite direction. It has
> generated a potentially dominating technology in
> search of a guiding philosophy.
> —HENRY KISSINGER[1]

A technology strategy is not the thing that will make or break your business. Technology is one tool in an arsenal of tools that can help make your business more efficient, more employee-friendly, and more customer-friendly. Technology is among an assortment of tools that help bring the customer experience mindset to life.

Here's the thing with companies and technology. Have you ever seen that inspirational quote "start before you're ready"? It was meant to inspire newbies to take a risk and try something even if they felt nervous to. However, companies that are looking to save a buck took this inspirational phrase to the extreme. Every day customers are accosted with half-baked technology solutions released before they should have been. Phone tree technology, chatbots, even checkout technology at the store: companies save money at the cost of the customer experience. Technology can create incredible experiences, but those experiences must be vetted and thoughtful, not simply thrown at customers.

A customer-focused company will always think of ways to make the technology experience of both the employees and the customers more seamless and zero-friction. Companies that do not have a customer experience mindset will find their technology strategies make the lives of these two groups harder, not easier.

One obvious question is why is there a gap between what the business needs and the technology delivered? One answer is simply communication. How adept is IT at understanding the needs of the business, and vice versa? Teamwork among your leaders is critical (as we'll read more about in chapter 7 on digital transformation).

Technology has become a critical piece of internal business conversations. There are a lot of reasons why technology can be a difficult conversation. One big reason is legacy—many companies are operating on outdated technology that does not integrate with the rest of the company's needs.

The new category of technology that impacts your customer experience is now called CEM, or customer experience management. Vendors like Adobe have helped shape this new category. Content management systems, marketing automation, analytics, CRMs and data sets, enterprise resource management systems (ERPs), cloud software, middleware, and other technologies need customer experience management to integrate well for optimal performance. The customer experience management market is projected to grow from an estimated $5.98 billion in 2017 to $16.91 billion by 2022.[2]

For years people have been talking about customer relationship management systems, but today CRM is table stakes (even though some companies still struggle to get their CRM in order). Due to advances in cloud software, AI, machine learning, and other digital software, companies can now operate at an elevated level, better serving both customers and employees. Technology decisions today must be made across the business.

An important part of your technology program is your employee experience.

Most painful customer experiences occur because employees do not have what they need to meet the customer's expectations. Research from Sharp has revealed that almost forty minutes per employee per day are wasted in UK offices, costing businesses over £2,100 per employee per year.[3]

US businesses lose up to $1.8 billion in wasted productivity each year due to obsolete technology.[4] Internal employee technology experiences matter a great deal, and are a critical part of the conversation of customer experience technology.

We have talked a lot in this book about employee experience, and how companies struggle to provide employees consumer grade technology experiences. Employees get incredible consumer technology experiences in their personal lives from companies like Spotify, Netflix, Amazon, and apps. Then they go to work and the technology experience is cumbersome. We need to think about the horizontal customer experience. When we have too many stops and starts for our employees internally, customers experience those stops and starts as well. Companies with better technology experiences also tend to boast happier, more engaged workers, which impacts the customer experience. Nearly 80 percent of employees who work at companies with "significantly above average" customer experience in their industry are "highly" or "moderately" engaged, compared with only 49 percent at companies with "average" or "below average" customer experience.[5]

When a company's organizational structure is optimized to serve the customer who expects a horizontal customer experience, the employees also enjoy a seamless experience. It is no longer suitable to create a siloed channel-centric organization. That means employees share data across the company. Every company today must embrace digital transformation. We cannot simply hire a chief customer officer, or appoint a customer experience group and think we are done. We must organize our companies with the thought that every single employee touches the customer experience in some way, and give them the technology and the tools to work with that customer experience mindset. IT has unprecedented authority inside the company to shape both employee and customer experiences. Research shows 89 percent of companies expect their IT budgets to grow or stay the same in 2019. Across all company sizes, organizations that expect IT budget increases next year anticipate a 20 percent increase on average, up from 19 percent in 2018.[6]

Every company today must be a data and technology company, but also think about e-commerce and how to create digital buying experiences. Customers are using social media, getting ideas on their phones, and want shoppable content they can immediately click through. As you think about the digital experience you offer customers, you can think about the ways new technology like artificial intelligence and machine learning fit into your digital strategy, like using computer vision to help customers identify what they're looking for. For example, Wayfair, the online furniture retailer, allows customers to take a photo of any item and find a similar item on the Wayfair website or app.[7]

Digitally native companies tend to be technology-first companies that provide innovative customer experiences. According to *The Economist*, seven of the world's ten most valuable companies by market capitalization are technology firms. Apple (which makes money by selling pricey gadgets) and Microsoft (selling software and services) are the exceptions. The other companies are built on a foundation of tying data to human beings. Finding out as much as possible about users' interests, activities, friends, and families is the focus of Facebook and Google. Amazon has a detailed history of shopper behavior. Hundreds of millions of Chinese use Tencent and Alibaba as digital wallets; both know their consumers well enough to provide widely used credit scores.[8]

Customer-focused companies think of technology as part of their customer experience strategy, always looking for ways to make customers' lives easier and better. A technology strategy is nonnegotiable.

In the past, customer experience technology meant contact center technology, which would include any technology that operates your call centers. Today, customer experience management is much more expansive; the new cross-channel customer demands experiences that follow across digital, phone, and in-person channels. Companies are often limping along to simply keep their customer service operations alive, and have struggled, often underresourced, to deal with volume. But now artificial intelligence and machine learning promise to deal with the mundane customer issues so companies can focus more on high-level customer experiences. While AI is still somewhat nascent, it's gaining traction as a serious part of any company's technology strategy.

HOW FAR AWAY IS WIDESPREAD ADOPTION OF ARTIFICIAL INTELLIGENCE?

Gartner predicted that the majority of customer service interactions would be automated by 2020, that you would have more interactions with a bot than with your own spouse.[9] But this prediction has not unfolded as Gartner thought it would. Even when robots can manage much of our customer experiences, will customers be happier without the support of a human? According to a recent report from PricewaterhouseCoopers, 75 percent of consumers say they want more human interaction in the future, not less.[10] There are some things we do not need a human to help us with, especially transactional experiences such as transferring money, finding a restaurant for dinner, or booking a flight. Robots can help our businesses with transactional and operational issues and make our businesses more efficient. That does not mean we are forecasting a world without people.

WHAT IS ARTIFICIAL INTELLIGENCE?

Artificial intelligence is a broad term used to describe machines programmed to think, work, and react like humans. Nearly three-quarters of decision-makers believe that AI will be the biggest business advantage of the future. Machine learning is when a device or software is trained to perform a task and improve its capabilities by processing information so the machine can learn over time. Due to recent advances in deep learning, which uses artificial neural networks that function like the human brain, the application of machine learning and artificial intelligence has improved.

Artificial intelligence is slowly making its way into many aspects of society, including autonomous vehicles, education (adapting content based on the individual student so the student can learn faster), retail (predicting the product the customer will buy next), manufacturing (you will hear more about how AI can help us identify factory issues in chapter 7), and finance (algorithms that predict the best trades). A robot is a machine that can do work by itself. Not all robots are smart, but a smart robot can be trained to carry out difficult tasks that require thought and adaptation. Global investments in robotics will surpass $180 billion by 2020, more than double what it was in 2016. By 2020, there will be more than 40,000 robots helping businesses around the globe.[11]

If we simply follow the money, the investments going into artificial intelligence are astounding. Forrester Research estimates that the "Cognitive Computing Technologies" (platforms based on artificial intelligence) business will be worth $1.2 trillion by the year 2020, with investments in AI tripling by then.[12] The power of machine learning and artificial intelligence today is its ability to sift through millions of pieces of data and identify patterns or key insights faster and better than a person could. AI has made its way into customer service in a variety of ways, including chatbots that are either customer facing or employee facing, improved personalization, and gleaning insights from data.

WHAT IS ROBOTIC PROCESS AUTOMATION?

Robotic process automation (RPA) is software that can be made to perform the kinds of administrative tasks that otherwise require tedious human effort—for example, transferring data from multiple input sources like email and spreadsheets to systems of record like ERP and CRM systems.[13] RPA provides businesses with the ability to reduce staffing costs and human error. A supercharged kind of RPA involves injecting RPA with cognitive technologies such as speech recognition, machine learning, and natural language processing, automating higher-order tasks that in the past required the perceptual and judgment capabilities of humans.

For example, Unum is a Fortune 500 insurance company that had a lot of legacy IT systems and lots of manual processes. They deployed Pega Robotic Automation to simplify their customer service, improve processes, and reduce costs. Using RPA, they automated 50 to 80 percent of the steps with customers, which took a great burden off the staff and enabled them to better serve customers.

Radial is a BPO running customer care operations for many top companies. They deployed Pega Robotic Automation to help streamline the work of their four thousand customer service reps across five customer care centers by eliminating the need to navigate across different systems to serve the customers. They reduced handle time by thirty seconds and improved first contact resolution by 6 percentage points.

COGNITIVE COMPUTING:
HELPING EMPLOYEES HELP CUSTOMERS

The difference between cognitive computing and artificial intelligence is the human element. Cognitive computing gives information to the human to make the best decision, while AI simply serves up the "best" answer. A chatbot that interfaces with a customer is an example of artificial intelligence, as are voice-activated assistants such as Amazon's Alexa, Google Home, Samsung's Bixby, or Apple's Siri. More than half of people already have a voice-activated assistant and use it.[14]

Many integrations with voice activated-assistants now allow you to engage in transactions with companies, such as transferring money between accounts, or finding out information about your insurance policy. You can plan a vacation using Alexa and do an array of other tasks such as control many of the IoT (internet of things) enabled technologies in your home. A voice-activated assistant is extremely helpful when your hands are busy, and research shows that 77 million US adults use voice assistants in their cars at least monthly, compared with 45.7 million using them on smart speakers.[15]

One of the major players in cognitive computing is Amelia from IPsoft, a cognitive agent used by Allstate. Amelia is trained on more than fifty unique insurance topics and regulations across all fifty states. Today Allstate uses Amelia internally, but in the near future they could be using it externally. Allstate employees ask Amelia to get concise answers about complicated insurance questions from customers. This cuts down on training time for employees and gets customers answers right away. (Slow customer experiences often occur because agents are working in slow software programs.) Representatives chat with Amelia while the customer is on the phone to get accurate information to the customer quickly. In an industry where regulations and compliance are incredibly important, Amelia helps make sure every customer's needs are met and are in compliance. Amelia provides the best of both worlds—the quickness and accuracy of AI mixed with the personal touch of human interaction. Amelia handles more than 250,000 conversations each month and is used by more than 75 percent of Allstate call center employees.

To give you a sense of how AI can create customer efficiencies, brands like Starbucks are using AI in their stores. Customers can chat with the My Starbucks Barista app to place their order with voice or text. When the customer gets to their local Starbucks, the order will be waiting and they can skip the line.

At Sam's Club (owned by Walmart) the warehouse superstore recently opened a smaller, AI-powered version of its store called Sam's Club Now, where customers can shop without having to go through a traditional checkout line. The corresponding app can even map the most efficient route through the store to get everything on a customer's shopping list.

Walmart is testing shelf-scanning robots in dozens of its stores. The robots scan shelves for missing items, things that need to be restocked, or price tags that need updating. The robots free human employees to spend more time with customers and ensure that customers aren't faced with empty shelves.

You can't talk about artificial intelligence and retail without mentioning one of the first functioning robot-driven grocery stores. I visited the Amazon Go store in Seattle and bought chocolate and an "Amazon" designed bottle. To be able to buy something at the Amazon Go store you must first download an app and scan the app on a barcode when you enter. Customers can simply walk into the store, take what they want from the shelves, and walk out without going through a cashier. Sensors and cameras throughout the store track what customers purchase, and their Amazon account is charged when they leave. AI helps create a quick and seamless shopping experience.

AI AND IOT

Artificial intelligence will be functionally necessary to wield the vast number of IoT devices, and will be even more important in making sense of an almost endless sea of data streamed in from these devices.[16]

The internet of things has evolved in the last few years in areas like telematics, logistics, and manufacturing. One example of how IoT is being used with AI is grocery chain Kroger, which is testing out the idea of smart shelves. When a customer walks down the Kroger aisle with their Kroger app open, sensors highlight products the customer might be interested in. The app could highlight foods that are gluten-free for a gluten-free shopper or kid-friendly snacks for a parent. The app also provides personal pricing and alerts shoppers if an item on their shopping list is on sale.

In the future, our cities will be smarter, with sensors on everything to help create more efficient ways to manage energy. The world is becoming more urban, with 60 percent of the population expected to live in cities by 2050. Across the globe, smart city technology is expected to grow to $135 billion by 2021, according to a report from the International Data Corporation (IDC).[17] A citizen might use a mobile app to avoid traffic jams, to find a parking spot, and to report a pothole or an overflowing dumpster. I moderated a panel last year at a conference called IoT World in Santa Clara, California, and met entrepreneurs who were working on sensors that help with refrigeration, logistics, putting sensors in a car for smart driving assistance, cloud-based infotainment solutions, automated emergency management, real-time fleet management, driver safety systems, and predictive maintenance.[18]

New research from IDC reports that the worldwide IoT market will grow to $1.7 trillion in 2020. IoT data can be used to greatly personalize the customer experience. IDC reports that worldwide revenues for big data and business analytics will grow from $130.1 billion in 2016 to more than $203 billion in 2020. With smartwatches and smart home gear, we are only seeing the beginning of this explosive market come to life. Increasingly we will see consumer products made "smart" and talking to other products to create an immersive technology experience for the customer.

An example of IoT comes from Carnival Cruise Line, which has created the first smart city at sea. Carnival operates more than 100 ships that travel to 740 destinations worldwide, and they're using a mix of IoT and AI to provide more tailored customer experiences.[19] The program is developed by Chief Experience and Innovation Officer John Padgett, the executive who developed Disney's $1 billion dollar magic band IoT program. The new IoT device for passengers is called the Ocean Medallion, and relies on 7,000 sensors placed throughout the ship. Every customer gets an IoT device that tracks their movements throughout the cruise ship and works alongside an app that serves up personalized recommendations for every passenger on 4,000 digital interaction points from 55-inch high-res screens distributed throughout every area of the ship. The goal is to provide as personalized an experience as possible. Through the IoT device, cruise ship passengers can set up their itinerary before departure, as well as check in remotely and connect to another Carnival technology called Ocean Ready, a paperless service that answers health questions and selects food preferences and various activities before passengers board.

Customers also can use their IoT device to access their room without a key because of geolocation technology. When a cruise ship passenger approaches their room, the door unlocks, the lights turn on, and the A/C adjusts to their preferred temperature. Clearly this is great for the passenger but also energy efficient for the cruise ship. Through the IoT devices, personal preferences are stored and guests receive invitations to special events and recommendations for what to do. The device allows customers to keep track of their children and other members of their group and offers intelligent navigation throughout the nineteen floors of the ship. Customers don't need money on the ship as they can charge purchases to their account through the IoT device. The goal was to create a personalized, seamless, and simplified experience while traveling.

THE SOFTWARE GLUE YOU ARE MISSING

One of the challenges for companies today is integrating internal technologies that now must talk to one another. Customers expect a zero-friction experience across the company, but they are not getting one. One of the culprits is disparate systems that aren't integrated: Thirty-year-old CRM systems do not play well with newer technologies. The experience hurts both employees who struggle with these old technologies and customers who experience many stops and starts.

Many companies sprint to fix their most visible issues first, followed by fixing channel by channel in a piecemeal approach. But McKinsey encourages companies to explicitly tie the reinvented customer experience to their operations. If they focus only on the front-end experience and don't change the back-end operations that support it, the new experience is unlikely to be sustainable.[20]

I first interviewed Glenn Laurie for my podcast when he was CEO of AT&T Mobility. He has since moved on to become CEO of Synchronoss, a publicly traded tech company that sells middleware to companies. We sat down while I was at CES so I could better understand his view on digital transformation. He said many carriers were really struggling with omnichannel and digital transformation. Digitization could enable telecom operators to improve their profits by as much as 35 percent if optimized for success, yet the average improvement achieved is just 9 percent.[21]

Most of us have had the clunky experience where an in-store telecom experience is on a different planet than the online experience. For many telecom providers, there is no such thing as omnichannel because the systems don't talk to each other. A digital company like Netflix has no problem with this because they built their entire business around a digital experience.

According to Laurie, becoming a more digital company is extremely hard to do and the only way is to "tear out" all the old systems. This is disruptive to the business and very expensive. Laurie said he is having tough conversations with retailers that started their life as a distribution point with locations. Now they want to be a distribution player and they can't make the transition. His clients tell him, "My customers are unhappy today. They can't start on the app and finish in the store. There is no continuity in the customer journey." A middleware layer can be one answer—a layer that sits on top of their systems. It is also known as "software glue," which can aggregate all customer touchpoints together. The goal for the company is higher customer satisfaction as a result of smoother customer journeys and an omnichannel customer experience. This improved digital experience results in lower contact center volume, which saves the company money.

In chapter 1, we talked about the customer experience mindset, and we talked about culture in chapter 2. Both of these things are huge assets for a digital transformation because change management can be a huge hurdle for big companies. Laurie gives an example: "If you're a massive retailer and you're good at physical retail and you try to go digital—which means change everything—it will fail." He says these programs fail not because the plan was wrong, but because employees don't buy in or make the change. He says the most important issue is to encourage your employees to make the shift. Culture is number one. "A lot of great companies have done all the right things except the culture and they've failed."

Laurie's views are supported by business research that shows disruption breeds tension, a result of a company's digital ambition conflicting with longtime operating objectives. This results in competing priorities and employees that don't know how to balance. An employee might be confused on what the priority is. Should they focus on speed or quality, innovation or efficiency? These are not easy problems to solve, and there is no one-size-fits-all solution.[22]

While Laurie espouses the benefits of digital, he believes physical retail will never die, and that customers still want to touch something in a retail environment. However, continuity between digital and physical is critical. Most of the business world is not operating at its full potential. Europe is currently operating at 12 percent of its digital potential, while the US is operating at 18 percent. Even within the leading economies of Europe, there are significant differences with Germany operating at 10 percent of its digital potential, and the UK at 17 percent. All over the world we are making our businesses vulnerable to customer churn by not creating more digitally fluid experiences throughout the organization.[23]

Customer Experience Technology Lessons from Glenn Laurie

- Integration of technology systems is critical.
- Customers today should be able to start in the retail store and finish in the app (and vice versa) with no trouble.
- Middleware—software glue—can help solve integration across your systems.
- Culture is the number one challenge for organizations undergoing a digital transformation.
- Ensure clear communications in change management as technology experiences for employees change.

Digital experiences have taken a front-and-center role in our personal lives. Companies that are slow to realize this are in for a wake-up call.

Many companies today, even if they say they value customer experience, show us by their behind-the-times digital experiences that they don't value customer experience. Nearly 60 percent of all consumers say companies have lost touch with the human element of customer experience (PwC Experience Matters report). Instead of leveraging technology to make customer experiences better, many companies have used half-baked clunky technologies to put a wall between themselves and their customers. For example, phone trees often lead you to a robot who still doesn't understand your query. The biggest offense is when companies tell you, "Due to higher than normal call volume, wait times are significantly longer." This means a company does not know how to staff up or staff down during peak times, or they don't want to spend the money on it. Customers today have choices, and they are increasingly choosing companies that differentiate on experience.

At home we enjoy the ease of use of technologies like Amazon, Apple products, Netflix, Spotify, and Uber or Lyft. Then we get to work and we are providing experiences to our employees and customers that don't compare to these consumer-grade technologies.

Thanks to innovation in cloud computing, artificial intelligence, machine learning, and big data, we have the ability to create better customer experiences. In the past, customer technology would simply mean the customer relationship management software you used to record the data of your customers for sales and customer service. But today, from voice-activated assistants to smart IoT-enabled products to entire virtual experiences offered to customers via their iPhones to a car that is run entirely on software (Tesla)—technology is a normal part of many customer experiences. Augmented reality now allows customers to try products and services virtually from their phone. Customers are starting to experience what it's like to want something and get it delivered instantly. Our products are starting to talk to us, understand what we want and need, and communicate that back to the company. Customers now expect real-time engagement, relevant and personalized experiences.

I am pro-efficiency. I believe we can build a world, assisted by technology, where life is simply more efficient. Most of the stuff we hate about common customer experiences could be improved with technology. Technology creates efficiencies, and efficiencies empower people. Efficiency allows us to spend more time doing the activities on earth we want to be doing. The companies that are creating compelling customer experiences with technology are doing so because they stop and think about the palpable impact they have on people's lives. They don't want to waste their employees' time or their customers' time.

We have the technology to actually improve so much of what our customers hate about the experiences we provide them. We have the technology to improve the way we communicate with customers, the way we anticipate their needs, and provide personalized and tailored experiences. We have the ability to provide our employees better technology, which has a palpable impact on the customer. Technology should be the thing that allows us to improve our businesses internally—allowing us to create more efficient and simple processes—with a downstream effect on our customers. However, the technology is often layered in a complicated mess inside the company, causing frustration for employees and customers who are the downstream recipients of that inefficiency.

THE CLOUD

Cloud technology has changed the game for customer experience, and our ability to provide better services to customers. Before we talk about how, let's get a quick overview of what cloud computing—a term we throw around frequently—actually is. Cloud computing is a metaphorical term for hosted services on the internet.[24] The availability of high-capacity networks, low-cost storage devices (as well as the widespread adoption of hardware virtualization), service-oriented architecture, and autonomic and utility computing has led to growth in cloud computing.[25] Cloud computing is done in massive data centers, as big as a handful of football fields. To give you an idea, Google has approximately 900,000 servers. The servers are small computers (think of a stripped-down motherboard from a laptop computer, plus a hard drive) stacked into towers.[26]

In the past, companies had individual clouds for their marketing and sales efforts as a way to pull together data, with each cloud holding information for just one area of the company. Today, the business world must push for a better way to manage the customer journey, and part of that is the way we store customer data.

The "experience cloud," as it is often referred to, brings together customer data, digital experience, and personalization to create a more efficient, modern way to monitor and interact with customers. The experience cloud is the infrastructure that allows brands to create useful, smooth experiences for their customers. One of the problems we've discussed in this book is that customers shop our companies horizontally, expecting one experience across products, devices, and retail experiences. However, our companies are set up vertically, by channel, and data sharing is an issue. The customer experience cloud creates a single 360-degree view of the customer by building bridges among marketing, customer service, sales, and other business groups.

The worldwide public cloud services market is projected to grow 17.3 percent in 2019 to a total of $206.2 billion, up from $175.8 billion in 2018.[27]

Even more granular, the contact center market for the cloud is expected to grow from $6.8 billion in 2017 to $20.93 billion by 2022.[28] A recent study revealed 73 percent of organizations have at least one application in the cloud, and another 17 percent plan to in the next twelve months.[29]

The experience cloud allows the company to pull in customer data from multiple sources, including websites, social media, and internal data to create a comprehensive customer profile. The cloud has a big impact on marketing, where in the past marketers had to work in and out of ten tools to get data on what customers were thinking, methods of communication, and product insights. With the cloud, companies can integrate across the business and gain a full view of the customer.

Amazing customer experiences happen when customers have to do very little work. With the cloud, companies can create seamless conversations and interactions across the entire customer journey, pulling everything together to create a better experience for the customer.[30]

Amazon Web Services (AWS) offers self-service cloud-based hosting, making it easy for companies to scale up or down. Amazon Web Services is a $17 billion a year business, serving customers like Netflix, Pinterest, NASA, and the CIA. Sandy Carter is a VP of Amazon Web Services, and an influential voice in the technology world. She spoke with me over the phone about Amazon Web Services, and how the cloud has paved the way for customer experience.

She said in the past, IT was a huge cost for small companies, and start-ups would burn through their cash spending funding on their servers. But with cloud technologies, they can spend less on storage, and spend more time on what Carter calls "core competencies." The power and reputation of AWS is the ability to scale up or down easily, the self-service nature of the platform, and the on-demand capacity because you only pay for what you use. Carter says that the hard part is actually "being able to use the data for insights." Most companies have a ton of data but it's not actionable and they don't know what to do with it. Carter said, "Data is the oil and insight is the power of the data, the refinement of that data."

One client of AWS is Capital One. They also focus on technology and innovation as a key differentiator. In 2010, CEO Richard Fairbank—whom we discussed in chapter 2—predicted that banking in the future would require a different technology organization, a different way to deliver, and a different way to succeed. He set out to be digital, to focus on three things: culture, customers, and technology. As described in chapter 2, Capital One focused on creating a culture based on trust, and they enjoy a strong reputation for innovation. Carter said Capital One began leveraging AWS and the cloud to go through their digital transformation. Capital One's mobile banking app was built with AWS, in addition to a new program for cyber claims, a new security model to operate in the public cloud rather than a database.

Peloton Bike is another company that has focused on customer experience, seeing explosive growth of over a million users. A Peloton bike is a stationary bike complete with a screen featuring a variety of classes you can take that are happening in real time. The bike is not cheap ($2,245) and classes are $39 a month. However, Peloton has a community of superfans totaling over a million users. The community is a major focus for the brand that launched with AWS in 2013. Part of the fun is the leaderboard, and the shared experience of joining other riders in an exercise enjoyed from the comfort of your own home. To be able to expand and scale this real-time experience, Peloton leaned on cloud services. They hosted a "turkey burn" during Thanksgiving in the United States with 20,000 requested views of the class per second. Peloton hosted an Olympic ride with up to 30,000 riders. Without the cloud, Peloton could not have supported the leaderboard experience.

In this chapter, we've explored the growing customer experience management space. Technology in this area will only continue to improve, as we become better stewards of our relationships with our customers. From software to robots to gadgets to how we store data, technology has become an important tool in our efforts to provide zero-friction customer experiences. In the next chapter, you will learn how many of these technologies have been applied to digital transformation, and how you can think about becoming customer-focused when it comes to the technology decisions you make at your organization.

7

DIGITAL TRANSFORMATION

> If you do not change direction, you may end up
> where you are heading.
> —LAO TZU[1]

Individual transformation can be hard, let alone business transformation. Digital business transformation often requires a steep learning curve for executives. In fact, 93 percent of executives say they know their industry will be disrupted at some point in the next five years, and only 20 percent feel they're highly prepared to address the threat of disruption.[2] Transformations today are required for businesses to remain afloat, because customers today are getting unprecedented experiences from digital-first companies like Amazon, Netflix, Spotify, Apple, and Uber, and comparing every other experience they have to those experiences.

Digital transformation is about using technology to solve traditional problems. It enables us to provide unprecedented value to the customer and continually evaluate how we do that. In a digital transformation, digital technology is integrated into every area of the business, including sales, product, marketing, and service. Digital transformation should aim to create a more seamless experience across the company.

The phrase "digital transformation" is misleading, because a transformation has a beginning point and an endpoint. But in today's world there are critical shifts in consumer behavior, and the technologies that customers use are changing every few years. In most cases digital transformation is handled by marketing, or another internal group such as IT. However, if you believe every division has an impact on customer experience, suiting one group up at a time doesn't make sense. If you want the customer experience to be seamless, the employee experience must be seamless. According to a survey in *Harvard Business Review*, more than 66 percent of CEOs said they expect their companies to change their business model in the next three years, with 62 percent reporting they have management initiatives or transformation programs underway to make their business more digital. Yet the same survey found that 72 percent of corporate strategists said their company's digital efforts are missing revenue expectations.[3]

The research shows that companies believe they need a digital transformation, and quickly, but they don't know where to start. Research shows 85 percent of enterprise decision-makers say they have a time frame of two years to make significant inroads into digital transformation or they will fall behind their competitors and suffer financially.[4]

The new normal for companies is a state of perpetual digital transformation—the digital environment. Every company must be able to evolve and pivot as the customer changes. Companies are very slow to achieve digital transformation, but what's actually required is that they embrace it as a permanent state of mind.[5] Simply saying digital transformation is a priority isn't enough.

Digital transformation works. According to Harvard Business School, digital "leaders" have a three-year average gross margin of 55 percent, compared to 37 percent for digital laggards.[6] But in order for digital transformation to be effective, it must be long term and involve every employee. This isn't a short-term initiative that will be replaced by another trend next year—this is the new normal.

DIGITAL TRANSFORMATION:
SOLVING TRADITIONAL PROBLEMS WITH TECHNOLOGY

CUSTOMER FOCUS
over product focus in technology decision-making

INTERNAL CUSTOMER EXPERIENCE
employees have consumer-grade technology

ORGANIZATIONAL STRUCTURE
that supports a seamless customer experience

LOGISTICS AND SUPPLY CHAIN
improve efficiencies

CHANGE MANAGEMENT
and cultural transformation

DATA SECURITY, PRIVACY, AND DATA ETHICS
standards are a focus

TRANSFORMATIONAL
leadership drives technology decisions

EVOLUTION OF PRODUCTS, SERVICES, AND PROCESSES
around delivery

TECHNOLOGY DECISIONS
involve entire C-suite

DIGITIZATION
of the business

INTEGRATION
of all data systems

PERSONALIZATION
guides the customer

DIGITAL TRANSFORMATION: SOLVING TRADITIONAL PROBLEMS WITH TECHNOLOGY

We are still at the beginning of this new era in technology. It is important for businesses to start working on their transformations now rather than wait longer. The first step into becoming a company that will survive the next wave of disruptions is understanding the role of customer experience. Today we must start making decisions in our organizations that are customer-focused over product-focused decisions. Companies like Adidas that obsess over customer experience outperformed the S&P 500 by more than 25 percent over a six-year span. Conversely, companies that failed to improve the omnichannel experience fell by more than 30 percent over that same time period.[7]

When you start to realize what is best for the customer, you soon realize you have to begin with equipping your employees with what they need to do their jobs. We are making our employees' lives miserable because our companies are not structured for them to thrive. Often employees are not equipped with what they need, whether it's information, tools, or connecting to other people in the organization who can help them.

Organizational structure must first be addressed before setting out on a digital transformation. The transformation requires a culture that is at times transparent, and embraces change. In 2016, organizational structure rocketed to the top of the agenda among senior executives and HR leaders worldwide, with 92 percent rating it a key priority.[8]

Your employees must be able to cater to modern customers. Without the structure in place, that will never happen. You can give your employees the best technology possible, but if they don't understand why the organization must change, and why it's good for them personally, they aren't going to buy in. Many digital transformations fail because employees do not support them. We heard about the challenge of culture in the last chapter as well. Change management is an overlooked aspect of digital transformation. As we learned in the introduction, people are wired to stay the same. Researchers at McKinsey highlighted the critical part change management plays in driving successful outcomes. But McKinsey's research found that most change management efforts fail because outdated models and change techniques are "fundamentally misaligned with today's dynamic business environment."[9]

We learned about transformational leadership in chapter 3, exploring the qualities of customer-focused leaders. Change is hard for people, and in times of change, people need strong leadership that makes them feel secure. Employees impacted by change are more than twice as likely to suffer from chronic stress.[10] Transformational leadership must make people feel moved to action, and part of something bigger than themselves.

Technology decisions cannot be made in a vacuum. All C-level executives must be involved. In the past, enterprise technology purchases involved, on average, 15.5 people in a purchasing organization. Half of these employees are within the IT department and the other half are within individual lines of business.[11] But heads of business units cannot always see across the organization. C-level executives have the visibility to buy and integrate technologies that provide the seamless experiences throughout the organization required today. A thou-shall-follow attitude in the technology office—as we learned from the CTO of Sephora— will not work. The CTO and CIO must learn the needs of the business by sitting down with the other leaders, and understanding their pain points and challenges.

Data must be a focus of your digital transformation, and companies must create fewer data storage systems in order for employees to actually be able to do something with the data. Data-driven organizations are twenty-three times more likely to acquire customers, six times as likely to retain customers, and nineteen times as likely to be profitable as a result.[12]

The bigger the company, the more complicated the approach to data. A data strategy that simplifies things is a must for any digital transformation. Unless your employee experience is seamless, including toward data, your customer experience will not be seamless. Today's employees expect the same consumer-grade technology at work that they enjoy in their personal lives.

Your employees are your first customers. What is their technology experience? Workers at technology laggards were 450 percent more likely to want to leave to go work elsewhere.[13]

In the next few pages you will read about companies that underwent digital transformations. In the age of Amazon, a digital transformation requires a better e-commerce experience, and that requires a look into the supply chain and logistics of your organization.

Efficiency is the future—how will you improve your supply chain and logistics to be smarter about how you get your products into the hands of customers? In a recent survey it was found that reducing costs and enhancing the customer experience were leading motivations for supply chain innovation (both at 31.4 percent), according to executives worldwide surveyed in March 2018 by eMarketer.[14]

Every day we hear about another data breach. Customers need to be able to trust their data is safe with your company or they won't ever give it to you. Nearly 60 percent of customers believe their personal information is vulnerable to a security breach. Customers today don't trust brands, and 54 percent of customers don't believe that companies have their best interests in mind.[15]

When customers give you their data, they expect a personalized experience in return. Personalization gets more important as generation Z grows up. Studies show 44 percent of generation Z customers will provide their personal data to enable a more personalized experience over an anonymous one. Additionally, 44 percent of generation Z would stop visiting a website if it did not anticipate what they needed, liked, or wanted.[16]

Digital transformation is the use of technology to solve traditional problems, but it also requires a change in thinking about how you deliver products and services, and even the products and services themselves. Today, our products are becoming smarter—for example, the Tesla car that continues to update itself through software. This is the future. Your product innovation and management must always consider how customer demands are changing, and be ahead of the curve. The evolution of delivery is key.

While Amazon has changed the game in many product categories, other companies are happily carving out their own piece of the digital pie with transformations, including Best Buy, Target, Sephora, 1-800-Flowers, and a discussion of B2B digital transformation.[17]

BEST BUY TRANSFORMS BY USING ITS WEAKNESSES AS STRENGTHS

Some companies' lack of digital presence is a problem. But for digital retailers, at times a lack of real estate and physical space is the problem. In fiscal 2012, Best Buy management said its struggles to grow revenue and profits were not just temporary "headwinds," but a result of the consumer electronics retail business's permanent shift. There was no sugarcoating it: Best Buy was in trouble. The company launched a "renew blue" strategy, which included the following five areas:

1. Reinvigorate the customer experience.
2. Attract "transformational leaders" and energize employees.
3. Work with vendors to innovate and drive value.
4. Increase the company's ROIC (return on invested capital) by growing revenue and efficiency.
5. Make the world a better place through recycling efforts and giving people access to technology.

When most companies struggle, they stop taking risks. They shrink in boldness and investments. Best Buy did the opposite, making long-term investments in their core fundamentals. To reinvigorate customer experience, Best Buy focused on offering customers unique benefits and exclusive membership programs, and continuing to develop a "leading edge, multichannel shopping experience through a highly relevant and contemporized hub-and-spoke network."

Best Buy's invested capital turns, or the revenue per dollar invested in its business, have improved each of the past five years after their digital transformation, while Best Buy's peer group of Amazon, Costco Wholesale, eBay, Kohl's Corporation, The Home Depot, Target Corporation, Walmart Inc., and Office Depot are making less revenue per dollar of invested capital. Best Buy stopped hemorrhaging money. After the digital transformation, cash on hand increased from $1.2 billion in fiscal 2012 to $3.1 billion in fiscal 2018. Best Buy cut its property, plant, and equipment (PP&E), lowering its debt significantly. All of these efforts made Best Buy more efficient and agile, enabling the company to better compete.

Best Buy proved that it was able to grow both its in-store and online sales, and find a mutually profitable relationship with Amazon. In the appliance and electronics markets, people still want to physically see and touch a product: Best Buy has something Amazon does not. They can benefit from one another, and recently Amazon and Best Buy launched a partnership to sell TVs powered by Amazon's Fire TV operating system. Best Buy will sell Toshiba and Insignia (Best Buy's private brand) TVs with Amazon's operating system in its stores and on its website. Best Buy will also be the exclusive retailer of these TVs on Amazon.com, so it doesn't risk simply being used as a showroom for online retailers. Customers can visit the Best Buy showroom and test the TVs in the store, but if they choose to purchase online, Best Buy still records that sale. In addition, Best Buy can sell customers additional products that integrate with Amazon's Fire TV and Alexa-capable products. The former CEO of Best Buy, Hubert Joly, said in a statement that "it's not a zero-sum game." Amazon cannot easily replicate Best Buy's showroom offering and Best Buy can provide value in a way Amazon currently can't. The company is focusing on the smart home market, enhancing its "geek squad" support, and improving customer service to meet customer needs.[18]

Lessons from Best Buy's Digital Transformation

▶ CEO leadership drives turnaround changes.

▶ Make long-term investments in core fundamentals.

▶ Offer customers unique benefits and exclusive membership programs.

▶ Clean up and lean out by focusing on efficiencies.

▶ Think of your business and how it can be complementary to Amazon.

TARGET TRANSFORMS ITS SUPPLY CHAIN AND IMPROVES CONVENIENCE TO COMPETE

Many expected Target to suffer because of Amazon taking an increasingly large share of its market, but Target's sales have been improving. Target, known affectionately by many as "Tar-zhay," is America's favorite department store. Almost 70 percent of Americans have a positive opinion of Target.[19]

Today Target makes almost $72 billion a year in revenue, but if they had not made some serious quick decisions on their digital footprint, they could be another Toys"R"Us. In 2003, when the internet became a "thing" companies realized they needed to reckon with, many companies simply outsourced to Amazon. This hurt companies that did not want to learn digital, and for some companies proved to be their demise. From 2003 to 2011, Target's website and fulfillment operations were managed by Amazon, and Amazon earned a commission on Target.com sales.[20] At the time, Target saw e-commerce as an ancillary service not worthy of much of their resources. After Target took back their website operations in 2011, they had some major hiccups, including their website crashing twice in six weeks.

The tenth largest employer in the United States with 350,000 employees, Target set out on a digital transformation, starting with its supply chain. Target integrated the store and digital inventories, developing the ability to fulfill online orders from local stores. Customers can now order items online and pick them up at the store. Hundreds of stores are also now providing miniature fulfillment centers, shipping items to customers' homes. This helps Target bring shipping costs down and get items to customers faster. Additionally, Target can fulfill orders online even when the item is "out of stock." This new supply chain approach has shifted the business, with 70 percent of Target's order volume fulfilled from its stores by November 2017.

Another convenient and customer-centric approach is a drive-up service where customers' online orders are brought outside and loaded into the car by Target staff in under three minutes. This is a service that digital-first companies like Amazon cannot currently do. Target is also making smart acquisitions to help with logistics such as Shipt, a delivery service company that will allow Target to make same-day deliveries and compete with Prime Now.

Not only is Target going through a powerful digital transformation and cleaning out the organization through a revamped supply chain and logistics, but Target focuses on its authentic in-house brands, and moving on from other in-house brands that felt outdated. Target's private labels have generated billions in sales for the company. For example, Merona and Mossimo were both brands that made the company money at one point, but felt dated. They had too many brands and none that stood out. Instead of trying to make them more appealing, Target gave itself the chance to simply start over and gave them up. Target released new brands such as Cat & Jack in 2016, which became a mammoth $2 billion brand, roughly as big as Lululemon Athletica.[21]

While other department stores get decimated, Target is standing strong. Target showed positive online growth in 2018, with online ordering (and picking up at a local store) surging 60 percent in November and December.[22]

Digital Transformation Lessons Learned from Target

- ▶ Revamp your supply chain so customers get items faster.
- ▶ Integrate store and digital inventories.
- ▶ Provide curbside pickup for shoppers.
- ▶ Focus on limited releases of authentic exclusive items only sold at your store.

A CUSTOMER-FOCUSED DIGITAL TRANSFORMATION AT SEPHORA

According to Deborah Yeh, Sephora's SVP of Marketing & Brand, the category of beauty is an always-evolving, immersive customer journey. In the past, the customer journey began and ended in the mall at the beauty counter, but today the journey can start on a variety of channels such as on the Sephora app or on social media. Sephora uses a phrase in their marketing, "Let's beauty together," and they see their experience as a two-way dialogue. Social media is a powerful force that connects the brand with millions of customers online.[23]

But Sephora hasn't simply used digital in their marketing, they use digital across the business to create efficiencies. Like other technology-first companies we'll talk about later in this book, Sephora collects app user behavior to make the customer experience more intuitive later. Through technology, Sephora can trace customer behavior all the way to the sale. They gather this information by analyzing the actions that a shopper takes after being presented with a product page. Sephora can later identify the customer's intentions. With this information they improve the personalization and customer journeys. They create a future experience that considers whether the shopper is researching and comparing products, planning a purchase for later, or ready to purchase a product immediately.[24]

Sephora has not been disrupted because they are in a constant state of digital transformation and disruption themselves. Sephora's customer experience is not easily repeatable because there is a strong connection between technology and brand. Other e-commerce brands that might try and disrupt Sephora do not have the brand that Sephora has. Sephora thrives because of an addictive inclusive culture internally and externally, and the sharp focus on creating a technology experience for a beauty customer specifically.

According to the *New York Times*, Sephora offers digitally savvy customers enough technological doodads and computer displays to make a Silicon Valley engineer blush.[25] Sephora's digital transformation is impressive, and they are leveraging emerging technology to sell products; however, the technology is not what is most significant. Bouhouch, Sephora's CTO, told me in our in-person interview, "It's not about just injecting digital, but it's about making a successful story." To make that happen, Sephora is looking at the feedback of data online and offline.

I am a Sephora customer and I can see my entire ten-year history with the company on my app. I can see they are using the data I've given them looking at my past purchases, my trips to the retail store when I've had my makeup done by an artist, and my web and app behavior as they are making real-time suggestions to me on what to buy next.

As the customer moves through Sephora's environments, the experience shifts in real time. But few companies have achieved this yet. Only 23 percent of companies are able to integrate customer insights in real time.[26]

Digital Transformation Lessons from Sephora

▶ Be a purpose-driven company.

▶ Think of your customer experience as a two-way dialogue.

▶ Use analytics to provide a real-time customer experience.

▶ Leverage a unique culture and tap into the employee base for inspiration.

▶ Create an innovation lab to find opportunities to improve the experience.

DIGITAL TRANSFORMATION AT 1-800-FLOWERS

1-800-Flowers is a public company with more than $1 billion in annual revenue, a company that embraced technology from its birth. Today, 1-800-Flowers's vision is to "Express, Connect, and Celebrate." Their mission is to "Deliver Smiles," and they do that by selling everything from bouquets to chocolates to fruit bouquets and popcorn. The company has always been a first-mover to technology, from their first 1-800 number in the 1970s, to selling products over the internet in the early 1990s, to today offering smart ordering capabilities from Samsung's voice-powered digital assistant, Bixby. They also offer voice- and chat-optimized capabilities on Google Assistant, including real-time auto tracking and search and shop features in the 1-800-Flowers store on Google Express. Additionally, on Apple Business Chat, a customer can complete text ordering and tracking capabilities by Apple Business Chat and upgraded search and shopping capabilities on the 1-800-Flowers bot for Facebook Messenger, featuring Track My Order functionality.

They think about how technology would best serve the customer, including a customer who might have forgotten to buy flowers in time for a special occasion, and get the product to the recipient in the most seamless, zero-friction way.[27]

Several years ago, 1-800-Flowers set out on a digital transformation to get all its fifteen subsidiaries under one roof. They started a loyalty program encouraging customers to shop across the brands on a single website where they can get free shipping and other loyalty offers.

The company has continued to thrive by capturing a large part of the "expression" market. For 1-800-Flowers the company wants to do everything it can to turn a customer into a multi-brand customer, which creates a loyalty very valuable for the company. When Jim McCann spoke of handing over the role of CEO to his younger brother Chris, he described him as someone who is always interested in technology. McCann wrote the forward for my last book, and I connected with him when he was a guest on my podcast to talk about the new Facebook Messenger chatbot for 1-800-Flowers. It's rare that a CEO is so involved in customer technology that he wants to talk about it with the press.

The company continues to push the envelope with technology. McCann told me in a phone interview for this book, "I think for us as a company right now our primary use of analytics is our focus on our customer database and our list." The company seeks to create a multibrand customer, and their technology strategies have aided in higher customer satisfaction and retention numbers than before.

Digital Transformation Lessons from 1-800-Flowers

- ▶ CEO helps drive technology strategy.
- ▶ Analytics are used to create personalized customer experiences.
- ▶ Customer journey is seamless and products are brought under one platform.
- ▶ Technology makes customers' lives easier, not harder.
- ▶ Multibrand customers, loyalty, and retention are earned by goodwill toward customers.

GLOBAL TRANSFORMATION FOR B2B

While buyers in the retail and consumer packaged good space get a lot of attention, when it comes to customer experience, often B2B is left out of the conversation, although there are more B2B companies in the world than B2C (business-to-consumer). Many B2B companies are product-centric rather than being customer-centric. They forget their buyers are using Netflix, Amazon, Spotify, and Apple products at home, and then at work are forced to use clunky technology experiences. Research also shows that B2B customers are becoming increasingly fickle. B2B customers hate a one-size-fits-all strategy.

The B2B company today must invest in becoming an experience-led business, which means optimizing every customer touchpoint.[28] The evolving B2B selling space, complex sales processes, and changing buyer expectations present new challenges for B2B sales teams.[29] Your B2B customer is just like you—they seek consumer-grade technology at work, but often don't have it in the sales or service process. Part of the problem is a lack of a customer experience mindset, as we explored in chapter 1. Only 14 percent of large B2B companies are truly customer-centric, where all employees are focused on the customer rather than their own product.[30]

CEB asked thousands of senior executives at companies around the world to describe the complex-solutions purchase process in one word. They came back with words like "hard," "awful," "painful," "frustrating," and "minefield."[31] The goal of making customers' lives easier and better isn't just for B2C companies, it's for B2B as well. Companies that anticipate customer needs and make buying easier are 62 percent likelier than other suppliers to win a high-quality sale.[32] For B2B buyers, one must consider what will make them more successful at work. The B2B buyer is more nervous and risk-averse than before. In the B2B space, vendors need to help B2B customers achieve their goals, but that doesn't simply mean asking them what they want. If you were to ask your B2B customers what they wanted, they might just say *lower prices*. To win more business you can act as a strategic partner helping the customer achieve long-term goals and suggesting strategies they might not be aware of. Recognizing the full range of emotional and rational factors behind business purchases—and then tailoring the value proposition—is a key strategy to avoid the commodity trap.[33]

We have to think of ways to personalize the customer experience, and not simply sell B2B businesses products and services they don't need. Customers are wary of overly aggressive salespeople, one reason why 59 percent of buyers prefer to research online rather than interact with a sales representative.[34]

In a B2B environment, how would Amazon, Netflix, or Spotify build experiences? They would create simple, intuitive, personalized, and flexible customer experiences—where the buyer can easily navigate from product searches through the purchasing process—and beyond, to aftermarket sales and service.

GLOBAL B2B TRANSFORMATION WITH TATA

Omnichannel customer experience is not just for the Apple customer. There is a great opportunity to transform the customer experience in large B2B companies, but legacy thinking and processes can be a huge hindrance. And management and culture can prohibit B2B companies from ever transforming themselves.

Dushyant Mohanty is the Global Transformation Head of Manufacturing, Energy, Banking, and Financial Services at Tata Consultancy Services. Tata is an Indian-based company with almost a million employees and $100 billion in revenue per year. Tata helps companies create transformation road maps and focus on people, process, and technology to get B2B companies there. Mohanty, who has been at Tata for twenty years, spoke with me via phone. He helps companies get out of "the shackles of being product-centric to become customer-centric" and helps companies understand what the implementation of a customer-centric strategy looks like.

He says one of the major challenges for B2B companies is how to bring change down to the level of operations, to set up processes and organizational structure around customer experience. Today there is potential for innovation in what is often a wasteful approach to service. Mohanty has seen how the internet of things can transform areas like manufacturing and supply chain, leveraging IoT in areas like commercial contracts design or service.

Mohanty cautions customers about the noise in the technology industry, vendors that boast "AI is baked into our product!" He says the next step is to consider your organizational structure and operations when it comes to being customer-focused and using technologies like AI and IoT to simplify areas of the business. He says B2B customers are fixated on things like driverless cars, but there is a spectrum when it comes to technologies. He helps companies create autonomous operations, but there are pieces that must be in place before the company can bring in the customer-focused technology.

There are new omnichannel customer experience requirements for B2B customers, and technology can help meet these new expectations. IoT can help eliminate waste and change the billing, contracts, and services processes, which often need to be modernized. Mohanty gives the example of a B2B jet engine maintenance repair and overhaul supplier company and an airline (which is the customer of the jet engine supplier). According to Mohanty, if you are an airline executive, in a product-centric world, your jet engine maintenance repair and overhaul supplier would provide you with services that included scheduled maintenance, parts, and labor. They would then bill you for services consumed. This is the power of IoT—there is less inefficiency and waste. In a customer-centric world, where IoT is enabled, customers now expect the manufacturers to bill only the flying hours of the engine. Moreover, the manufacturers are themselves using the customer intelligence and the performance of their assets to guide airlines in their parts commerce process—whether it is directly through their traditional selling channels or through new parts marketplaces in their sector.

Have you ever driven in a city downtown very early in the morning or extremely late at night and noticed many lights in business offices, but no one working? Today IoT sensors can help reduce waste in a variety of scenarios when the equipment does not need to be on, whether that's lighting, heating, or refrigeration.

One example is manufacturer Atlas Global Solutions who reduced energy costs by 75 percent and increased productivity by 20 percent[35] by using intelligent LED lighting systems from Digital Lumens.

Smart thermostats can save 15 percent or more on your annual energy costs. They do this by optimizing your home's heating and cooling based on the weather, your preferences, and the price of electricity at various times of the day.[36]

Another example of transformation in the B2B space is an HVAC (heating, ventilation, and air-conditioning) manufacturer. Their catalog items would include compressors, refrigeration, and commercial water tanks, which are usually sold by distributors. In the past, HVAC companies would provide those items through their distribution channels. But now, with the focus on IoT including smart buildings and energy-efficient infrastructure, customers expect to only pay for specific energy usage. They want efficient usage. These customers are now integrating their parts with other infrastructure providers. So the customer for a typical HVAC manufacturer has now expanded beyond the normal equipment buyer to facility managers and building general managers who are now part of the buying journey.

The old part distributor and manufacturing company has to transform their customer engagement journey from relying on a traditional distributor channel toward defining new customer experience journeys for buying their products and solutions. Analytics can help B2B suppliers predict and forecast outages or service needs. This is personalization on the B2B level, which provides a superior customer experience. According to Mohanty, HVAC providers have to forge new partnerships with other suppliers since the customer expectations are now outcome-based and the buying process is more immersive. Today, B2B customers demand mass customization, but many B2B companies are not equipped to deliver it.

Another challenge in B2B manufacturing is the change management piece. There can be conflicts with decision-makers that slow innovation. According to research, the most common reason for the high number of failures in digital transformation is that the required changes to the business model overwhelm the initiative.[37]

For example, all senior executives have different KPIs they need to hit. The head of the supply chain must deliver products and services on time. The CFO will protest a change in how customers are charged and serviced, because if the company is not equipped to deliver last-minute orders or service, the costs are going to increase.

Transforming how you sell and service customers can be difficult, but by focusing on being customer-centric over being product-centric in every decision, eventually you will get there.

Digital Transformation Lessons Learned from Tata

- B2B customers today expect customization.
- Transform your customer engagement journey away from relying on a traditional distributor channel and toward defining new customer experience journeys.
- Analytics can help B2B suppliers predict and forecast outages or service needs.
- IoT can help B2B manufacturing companies become more efficient.

➤ Ensure metrics are tied to customer experience.
➤ B2B operations, processes, and organizational structure all impact customer experience.

In this chapter, we've learned about digital transformation. We've looked at companies like Best Buy, Target, Sephora, and 1-800-Flowers, as well as heard from a B2B manufacturing expert to learn about trends in IoT and how IoT is transforming traditional sales channels. The new reality is that companies today must be in a constant state of digital transformation. We are all now data and technology companies that must think about the customer of the future. In the next chapter we'll take a look at personalization, and the role digital transformation plays in creating the zero-friction, seamless, and personalized experiences for tomorrow's customer.

8

PERSONALIZATION AND THE CUSTOMER EXPERIENCE OF THE FUTURE

> Figuring out how to scale the very human art of personalization is difficult, but I believe that it is also the key to building a lasting connection with customers for the long term.
> —KATRINA LAKE[1]

I t's 6:30 a.m. and the first thing I do upon waking is turn off the house alarm, let the dogs outside, and open my iPhone to check my Nest app to see if my two-year-old daughter is awake. I see on the camera she's still fast asleep—and I get a few more minutes to get my morning started. I feed the dogs, make some coffee, and open an app called Headspace. I use apps for meditation for ten minutes every morning to clear my head before my busy day of being a wife, mother, and entrepreneur. The meditation app knows me, so I rarely have to do much digging to find the right meditation for the moment. I simply click on the meditation served up.

When the meditation ends, I ask Alexa the weather and to play the local news for me. Fast-forward ninety minutes, everyone is awake and we have tackled morning responsibilities that include walking the dogs and driving our daughter to preschool. I grab my fourth technology experience of the day, a device sold to me by a fitness studio called OrangeTheory, where my workout is gamified. I sweat to accrue points displayed on a screen for me so I can track my progress as I work out. These workouts have motivated me to work harder because my effort is up on the screen for me and everyone to see. I can see if I am pushing myself hard enough or not by the color of my heart rate on the projected screen in the fitness studio.

After the class, I am sent a detailed analysis of my one-hour workout through the app and email. After getting myself ready, I open my fifth app of the morning, Spotify, to listen to some music while I check email and start my workday.

What shaped my morning? Technology experiences that enrich my life because of the extreme level of personalization. Increasingly, technology makes customer experience like those I mentioned above deliciously easy.

You know what I'm talking about because you, too, enjoy these apps and technologies in your own life. And while individually we know how technology can be incredibly powerful in helping us live a more enjoyable, seamless life—unfortunately at work when we build experiences for other people something goes wrong. We create mass experiences for our customers. Just 22 percent of shoppers are satisfied with the level of personalization they currently receive.[2] We simply have not had the technology in the past to scale personalization on the level required. But in the future, personalization will not be a luxury, but a requirement.

The challenge is that companies are focused on maximizing operational efficiencies to increase profits. That means one-size-fits-all experiences like the ones you get from industries like cable, internet providers, wireless phone service providers, healthcare, and the airline industries. These are the five most hated industries according to research from the American Customer Satisfaction Index.[3]

Think of what's happening in retail right now. While many department stores are currently going through digital transformations, the experience of shopping in a department store is still not a personal one. Going through a building remodel is not enough to retain customers. The entire model provides an impersonal customer experience. Shopping in a department store can feel daunting. The space is enormous. When you go to a department store, you do not always know what you want or where it would be located. However, it's the retailers that have gone through digital transformations, that provide compelling e-commerce experiences to support the retail store, that are thriving today. While digital is still simply a bite out of overall retail spend, the growth numbers are more significant than the total sales number. Early analysis from *Internet Retailer* shows online retail sales in the US crossed $517 billion in 2018, a 15 percent increase compared with 2017. In contrast, retail growth in physical stores reached only 3.7 percent last year. E-commerce now accounts for 14.3 percent of total retail sales. Only ten years ago, e-commerce was at 5.1 percent of total retail purchases.[4]

E-commerce and digital first companies will continue to shift this statistic. The traditional retail shopping experience is highly impersonal, the opposite of the ease of interaction and personalization a shopper can get online. More than half of millennial shoppers feel that store associates do not have the tools they need to deliver great customer service.[5]

When companies have gone through digital transformations, such as Nordstrom or Macy's, these transformations have lengthened their lives. However, the jury is still out if these transformations will carry these department stores into the future.

Some innovators are using artificial intelligence to provide more relevant and engaging retail experiences. For example, clothing designer Rebecca Minkoff is one of the first brands to create "connected stores." Rebecca Minkoff's three stores use AI to run touchscreen smart mirrors, which allow customers to browse through clothing items and inspiration. Shoppers can then try them on in an interactive fitting room with custom lighting options. The fitting room mirrors use RFID (radio-frequence identification) technology to automatically know what customers are trying on and tell them what other colors and sizes are available.

Findability is a big challenge in any retail experience. Luxury department store Neiman Marcus uses AI to make it easier for customers to find items. The "Snap. Find. Shop." app allows users to take pictures of items they see while out and about and then searches Neiman Marcus inventory to find the same or a similar item. Wayfair also enables this on their app, and visual search is becoming an increasingly critical type of AI. Instead of using vague search terms to find an item, the photos can usually find a very similar match. If you aren't sure where to find something you see, chances are you're going to shop at the company that helps you find it.

Easy curbside pickup is gaining traction for retailers who are competing with Amazon Prime's free two-day delivery. Fashion retailer Zara started using robots to help customers when they come to pick up their orders. When the customer enters the store, they enter a pickup code that starts the robot moving in the warehouse. Once the order has been found, the robot delivers it via a physical drop box. It's a quick and efficient way to get orders to customers who want items same day.

Customer feedback is critical to finding out how customers like to be served, and what they want. Recent studies from Forrester show that 39 percent of companies don't regularly ask customers for feedback about their interactions—the most basic form of CX measurement.[6]

Clothing store Uniqlo is pioneering the use of science and AI to create AI-powered "UMood" kiosks that show customers a variety of products and measures their reaction to the color and style through neurotransmitters. Based on each person's reactions, the kiosk then recommends products. Customers don't even have to push a button; their brain signals are enough for the system to know how they feel about each item. Today this is an advantage an in-store retailer would have over a website, although some customers might not want to use this invasive technology.

However, imagine how much faster this would be rather than taking your allotted items into a dressing room and having to call for the dressing room attendant to change out your items and tell them if you liked the items or not.

WE OFTEN HEAR ABOUT SEGMENTATION in marketing, but segmentation is the opposite of personalization. There is no point in constructing personas anymore, because what use is a persona when you actually can see your individual customer data at scale? Two people who have the same persona can have completely different actual behaviors. Your personal characteristics do not determine you will have a specific behavior in the future.[7] Even though I am a female millennial mom living in Northern California, I am very different than the thousands of other female millennial moms living in Northern California. Why are we still talking about personas and segmentation when we know they are often inaccurate?

Time is our most important commodity, and personalization respects customers' time. If you aren't in the business of saving your customers time, making their lives easier and better, you risk being disrupted by a newbie who will. Customers will defect to companies that know them, anticipate their needs, and provide just-in-time products and services. Companies won't notice this slow exodus until their market share is gone, and it will be too late.

The best customer experiences are built by individuals who see a problem and are able to see a better way. Today we have the data to create personalized customer experiences, and studies show customers would gladly give up some data to a trusted company in exchange for a desirable customer experience. For example, studies show 57 percent of consumers are willing to share personal data in exchange for personalized offers or discounts. A similar number of consumers would share personal data in exchange for product recommendations, or for personalized shopping experiences.[8] When customers trust a brand, the customer will exchange their data for value, but this relationship must be treated with white gloves. The minute a brand breaks the trust of the customer, that incident will forever bruise the relationship.

DIRECT TO CONSUMER

Direct to consumer companies have been disrupting markets at every turn. Forget the middleman: More companies are going straight to consumers with online brands. As they gain traction online, many of these companies are making the jump to physical retail stores, often with great success. Think about luggage and lifestyle brand Away (reached profitability in under two years); subscription-based razor company Dollar Shave Club (sold to Unilever for $1 billion); or Casper, which is upending the mattress industry ($100 million company in under two years). With a focus on convenient services, incredible content that caters to millennials, and personalized customer experiences, these companies are growing incredibly fast. Big retailers are jumping on the bandwagon, with more than 57 percent of manufacturers embracing direct-to-consumer (DTC) models, representing the fastest growing category in e-commerce. Nike has launched a major effort to focus on direct to consumer, predicting to grow DTC sales from $6.6 billion in 2015 to $16 billion in 2020.[9]

DOLLAR SHAVE CLUB: WE WANT TO SOLVE MEN'S PROBLEMS IN LIFE AND IN THE BATHROOM

Personalization is when a company treats a customer more like a person and less like a wallet. It's the customer experience mindset in practice, when the company makes life easier on the customer, even if it means making it harder on their own brand. It is what happens when the company leverages a deep understanding of customer preference, structured and unstructured customer data, conversations in and across all channels; when companies can preemptively anticipate a customer's needs. One great example of personalization is Dollar Shave Club. In the past, the process of simply buying razors was painful. To buy a razor in a store you had to ask an employee to unlock a case. Dollar Shave Club founders Mark Levine and Michael Dubin met at a party and shared stories of nightmare razor blade shopping. Dollar Shave Club first launched as a membership service on March 6, 2012, via a quirky, honest, and funny YouTube video that went viral. (Today it has almost 26 million views.) Dollar Shave Club was a quick success despite the unanticipated amount of traffic from that video crashing the company's server in the first hour. Once Dubin got the server working, he enlisted a team of friends and contractors to help fulfill the twelve thousand orders that arrived within forty-eight hours of launching the video.[10]

Social media is a natural content strategy for D2C companies, and if you are going to create a D2C subscription service, it should be for something people need consistently, such as razors. Customers love the irreverent marketing and convenience of getting something—formerly locked away in a case at a store— delivered directly to their door.

I interviewed Alan Wizemann, Dollar Shave Club's Chief Data Officer. Wizemann was formerly at Target, where he launched the widely successful Cartwheel e-commerce app. He later went on to become a VP of Guest Experience and Digital Product Management at women's fitness brand Lululemon Athletica. Wizemann considers himself a problem solver who focuses on efficiencies. He said, in a phone interview with me, that personalization is not just website technology. The key is to focus on the guest or the user, design great products, and tell amazing stories about them. He said, "Companies that do that at scale can hold their own." While Dollar Shave Club might seem like a basic offering, Wizemann and his team are thinking through the actual life of the customer, particularly in the bathroom. He says that Dollar Shave Club, by focusing on education, is providing an authentic experience Amazon cannot provide.

Wizemann talks about what he calls the "feel part of the service" in order to find the right product for the customer's problem. Wizemann says they want to focus on the problem for the individual, and you can't get that at a company that offers massive scale. The company focuses on personalized customer education, and they are constantly looking at lifestyle trends for men. But they don't stop there; they are looking at larger cultural trends and "humanity in general." Wizemann says the issues they look at are "way beyond what we consider a grooming company to play with—we are starting to use and incorporate this into our ecosystem." Dollar Shave Club wants to be a companion to the customer, guiding men who might feel frustrated with grooming in general.

The exciting part about data is we can use it to create incredible just-in-time experiences for customers. As Jamie Gutfreund, CCO of Hasbro, described to me, "Imagine you have a business trip coming up and your airline knows that you're a SoulCycle fan. Perhaps the airline could work with third parties to help design an experience for you while you're on your trip, even getting you involved in local SoulCycle classes, or providing other value adds that would make your trip better." Customers are willing to give up some data and privacy for experiences that are personalized, and make their life easier. I am not talking about how airlines will hound you with offers such as partnering with car rental companies and hotel companies. Companies that use customer data and analytics in an accountable manner—being transparent with customers—show measurable advantages, averaging an 11.2 percent year-over-year growth in their customer win-back rates, and an 8.1 percent increase in customer satisfaction.[11] Not only does responsible use of customer data benefit the company, but analytics plays a pivotal role in a company's ability to create goodwill with customers. Studies show that companies that use customer analytics average a 14.6 percent annual increase in positive mentions across social media channels.[12]

In the next chapter we'll be looking at analytics and how analytics can open up a new world of personalized experiences you can offer your customer.

THE POWER OF CUSTOMER EXPERIENCE ANALYTICS

9

> I'm a perfectionist. I'm pretty much insatiable. I feel
> there's so many things I can improve on.
> —SERENA WILLIAMS[1]

In your own life, your goals are important. In your job, you are held to performance goals. Through metrics or KPIs we have a gauge of where we are and how we are improving. Analytics is the discovery, interpretation, and communication of meaningful patterns in data, and the process of applying those patterns toward effective decisionmaking.[2]

Analytics informs our decisions about life at home and at work. On a basic level let's say you want to save up money to take that dream vacation you've always wanted, or you're saving up to buy a condo or home—you've got to look at how much money is coming in and how much money is going out. If you want to lose weight, you're going to look at what you're eating, and it helps to write it down so you can see it on paper or track your nutrition in an app. You're also going to consider how much you're exercising. The reason these markers are important is they make our goals tangible. In order to achieve *Y*, we have to do *X*. If we can't measure something, we cannot improve it. When it comes to work, not everything can be measured, but thanks to advances in artificial intelligence and our ability to recognize patterns in data, we are able to measure more than in the past. Today we can look at structured and unstructured data and identify patterns that can provide insights into customer experience. Analytics isn't challenging or complicated when it's a small pool of customers; however, if you have a company with millions of customers, it can be more complicated. This is where analytics can be your greatest strength. By 2020, more than 40 percent of all data analytics projects will relate to an aspect of customer experience.[3]

Today's technology arms you with tools to get smarter about your customers, where in the past we were stuck with blanket approaches. We relied on segmentation, building "personas" of our customers—but today we have technology that allows us to see the individual customer, and identify patterns across a diverse customer base.

In this chapter we are going to look at analytics in three ways. Firstly we'll explore a modern approach to calculating customer lifetime value (CLV), and how companies are measuring the value of their customers. We'll get specific about how a modern approach to CLV can help determine how and what they sell to customers, as well as using customer lifetime value to determine the future value of your business. We will look at predictive, prescriptive, and descriptive analytics, in practice. Third, we will look at how marketers can use analytics to make real-time bets on offers for customers.

HOW VALUABLE ARE YOUR CUSTOMERS?

Companies do not always admit that their relationships have varying values. They don't want to admit that some of their customers are more valuable than others. One way to calculate the value of our relationships is customer lifetime value.

The problem for businesses when it comes to customer lifetime value is many of our equations are past-looking rather than future-looking. A future-looking view allows you to know how valuable a relationship will be in the future. This way you know who to invest in and how. Peter Fader, who has been a marketing professor at Wharton for thirty-two years and spent a lifetime helping companies with data science, advises "customer centricity"—focusing on a small group of your most valuable customers and surrounding them with relevant products and services. His view is contrary to what most people think of when they hear "customer experience." He believes premium experiences should be saved for your valuable customers, and you must decipher through data and math who those are. When Fader is not teaching or writing books, he is working on estimating company value by predicting future customer behavior—acquisition, churn, and spending. He had a company called Zodiac that did this (and was acquired by Nike), and he is working on a new company called Theta Equity Partners that is innovating the current approach to corporate valuation.

Fader believes most companies are obsessed with volume and cost. Many companies are simply throwing things at the wall and hoping they stick. There are vanity metrics: For example, you could have 50 million users but you might not have a sustainable business model. Fader's suggestion is to find your best customers and look for ways to expand the relationship with them.

When it comes to CLV, Fader is trying to pivot the current conversation around customer experience and encourage the entire industry to change how we talk about customer lifetime value. He sees a modern approach to CLV as a way to help marketers and customer experience professionals get a better understanding of how to allocate their resources for the future, and applies his financial modeling to help create more accurate gauges of corporate valuation.

By focusing precious resources on the best customers, Fader suggests, we increase the likelihood of creating a profitable business, rather than spending our resources on everyone across the board. Part of the challenge is customer experience professionals often don't have the language or the tools to show decision-makers inside the company to show customer lifetime value. According to Fader, marketers shy away from analytics, and are "afraid of the future."

The idea of heterogeneity of customers makes sense; your customers are not all created equal, but they are all unique. In the past, analytics did not give marketers the ability to focus on the future, but focused strictly on the past. Now marketers have the ability to identify how valuable a customer will be. According to Fader, what people don't realize about customer experience is it is a finance question more than anything else.

If we figure out customer lifetime value, we can get the attention of the CFO. We will have more money for customer experience–focused programs. Fader does not believe marketing is a soft discipline, and he wants to better enable marketers to show the clear ROI of their customer programs. Being able to show the ROI of a customer initiative is an important aspect of this work, because this is the language of the CFO and the CEO, those who need to be influenced in order to get them interested in investing in customer experience.

When we step back and think about how we can gain greater support and resources for customer programs, we need analytics to actually prove the value of what we're doing to the people who carry the purse strings at the companies where we work.

It used to be that it cost a lot of money to acquire new customers—in fact, general business folklore is that it costs five times as much to create a new customer as it does to retain an established one.[4] We would sell customers through mass advertising and push selling. But today's world is based on change. As our customers' lives change, the way they perceive us changes. Our brand's place in the customer's world changes, and we must continually consider that as we sell to them. It makes more sense to focus on one area, get to know that customer base, and continue to sell them products and services that are relevant for them.

When it comes to customer centricity, Fader told me in a phone interview that CLV, when used right, can be a magic wand.

Customer lifetime value is a prediction of the net profit attributed to the entire future relationship with a customer. The prediction model can have varying levels of sophistication and accuracy.[5] Companies that focus on customer lifetime value tend to focus on the long-term relationship with the customer over the focus on quarterly profits.[6] Once you discover the future value of your customers, you can undergo a cultural transformation. You can focus on cross-functional alignment. The way you communicate internally and externally can be impacted. Fader believes companies can be challenged to bring a new vision to life in an organization historically built around product volume and cost.

But it's not enough to simply have the CMO won over; you have to get buy-in from across the organization. Fader says if you don't have absolute buy-in from the CFO and supply chain, it's just going to be the marketing flavor of the month.

When it comes to the best math to help a company focus on its strengths and become more efficient, customer lifetime value isn't the only factor. It's also about a new way to calculate the worth of a company, and Fader is now focusing on a new way to discover customer-based corporate valuation. He does this by predicting future customer behavior and calculating acquisition, churn and spending. Many of the world's most innovative companies financially do not look like what we're used to. We know Amazon blew through many millions before they became profitable. Netflix is billions of dollars in debt but has almost 150 million paying subscribers. Fader believes traditional corporate valuation methods often miss key customer-driven leading indicators of company value, which limits their accuracy. These methods are not focused on modeling the customer-related activity that generates companies' revenue. Traditional valuation is backward-looking, extrapolating off of historical financials and less diagnostic for growing companies with negative cash flows. Perhaps you are not the person at your company responsible for valuation; it's still something to think about as technology-first companies continue to set records, and business models of all kinds are disrupted by unicorns.

Analytics and CLV formulas can help inform our decisions across the business, and as our businesses access more data, we have more at our fingertips to understand where our resources should be going.

One thing is for sure—your customers are all unique, but we have to be strategic about our resources. We know it isn't smart to treat anyone poorly, but it does make sense to surround our most valuable customers with relevant products and services.

TWO BENEFITS OF PREDICTIVE ANALYTICS

Customer experience analytics helps companies operate with increasing accuracy, while also providing benefits to the customer. When we provide marketing with proper analytics, it can create more personalized experiences. According to research by McKinsey, when brands get personalization right, marketing spend can deliver five to eight times the ROI and lift sales by 10 percent or more.[7]

It makes sense for you as a customer, doesn't it? When someone remembers your name, or something you told them the last time you interacted with them, or some preference you have when you order your food, it makes you feel good. Most companies have total amnesia when we talk to them. They have no idea who we are, what we need, or what happened the last time we interacted with them. Analytics helps companies to be better listeners, to provide more relevant experiences, and to be where we are when we need their help.

Data is no longer a level playing field. The companies that are using machine learning and artificial intelligence software to scour their data have a leg up on companies that are simply using yesterday's approach.

As we learned from Professor Fader, looking backward can be our demise. In the past, data analysts would take a passive analytical "here is what happened" view. A report would be generated to show sample sizes of structured data from a silo within a system or corporate function.[8] Now, with machine learning and artificial intelligence, we can look forward, predicting the future to create more efficiencies in the way we run our businesses, and in the contextual, personalized experiences we move customers through.

There are many benefits of predictive analytics for both the company and the customer. With predictive analytics we can predict customer churn, create a preemptive service model, and anticipate customer needs. For example, FedEx is able to predict which of their customers will defect to a competitor with 60 to 90 percent accuracy.[9] Sprint is able to identify a segment of customers that is ten times more likely to cancel compared to the rest.[10] Most companies aren't leveraging our data as much as they could be. The numbers are shocking when you look at where companies access most data today. Most customer data comes from a customer relationship management system (75 percent). A distant second is data from customer satisfaction surveys (53 percent), third is data from social media tools (43 percent), fourth is feedback from sales and retail staff (40 percent), fifth is email or SMS (37 percent), and sixth, transaction data (34 percent).[11]

Unstructured data is found outside of these six channels. It can include documents, social media feeds, digital pictures and videos, audio transmissions, sensors used to gather climate information, and unstructured content from the web.[12] Today, 80 percent of all data is unstructured. We can't read it or use it in our computing systems. By 2020, that number will be 93 percent.[13] These are some of the tangential details that could provide a more holistic view of the customer.

There are three types of analytics for customer service: descriptive analytics, predictive analytics, and prescriptive analytics.

Descriptive analytics looks at raw data and asks the question "what happened?" In customer service, we learn what happened by looking at customer service key performance indicators (KPIs), customer satisfaction, amount of tickets, amount of resolved tickets, and more.

Predictive analytics predicts the future, and can include strategies like modeling, machine learning, and artificial intelligence. The results provide data-backed prognostication that can help business leaders better understand unknown, future occurrences.

Prescriptive analytics are when you ask the question "What can we do to make *X* happen?" or "What should be done?" Prescriptive looks at how you can control or create a future outcome and includes processes like graph analysis, simulation, event processing, machine learning, and heuristics (a practical method that might not be perfect or rational, but is sufficient to reach a goal).[14]

The difference between predictive and prescriptive is this: Predictive analytics forecasts what will happen in the future. Prescriptive analytics can help companies alter the future.[15] Predictive forecasts potential future outcomes, while prescriptive helps you draw up specific recommendations.

We established that through advances in artificial intelligence and machine learning we can do a better job of looking forward rather than looking backward. We can use predictive analytics to create that personalized customer experience that the customer craves. Predictive analytics have the ability to make our organizations more efficient, and create more frictionless customer experiences.

CAESARS HOTEL MAKES REAL-TIME BETS ON PREDICTIVE ANALYTICS FOR MARKETING

While in the 1990s and 2000s, over half of Las Vegas Strip revenues came from gambling, in recent years, gaming's share of the revenue mix has sharply declined. In 2017, only 33 percent of Las

Vegas Strip revenue came from gaming, while the rest came from growth in food and beverage, hotel, entertainment, and nightlife. Caesars has focused on evolving their product while also using analytics to make real-time offers to loyal customers. Caesars uses predictive modeling techniques to understand different customer scenarios, to see how much marketing encourages a trip versus serving as the icing on the cake of a trip someone would have taken anyway. Various real-time rewards could include a free hotel room, slot credit, golf, food, transportation, sold-out tickets, or a room upgrade. Other companies would ignore outliers, but for a casino like Caesars that could be a million-dollar customer.[16] Caesars actually has a fleet of five private planes for what they call "ultra VIP" guests, and have charter planes to take their best customers to various Caesars locations.[17]

Caesars is also using location data from customers received from its mobile app. The app offers the customer conveniences such as skipping check-in queues, making reservations, and ordering room service. Caesars can see where the customer is—meaning they can offer location-based promotions.[18] Data and analytics can set your brand apart: Customers today want just-in-time offers, and increasingly seek out experiences where the brand helps the customer make the most of the experience.

Real-Time Marketing Lessons from Caesars:

- ► What real-time offers can you make your customer?
- ► Consider what the customer is looking for from your experience, and how you can better meet their needs throughout the experience.
- ► Ensure you are evolving your product while simultaneously helping customers maximize the value of the product.
- ► Create special programs for your most loyal customers and surround them with relevant products and services.

GLAXOSMITHKLINE USES PREDICTIVE ANALYTICS FOR CLINICAL TRIALS

Everyone in the company impacts customer experience in some way. That is especially true for pharmaceutical companies, when scientists and clinical trial doctors also impact the customer's experience of the final product. In the United States, it takes an average of twelve years for an experimental drug to travel from the laboratory to your medicine cabinet, and costs $1.6 billion. Most people who need a drug due to serious illness do not have twelve years to wait. Bringing a medicine to market is extremely time intensive and resource intensive. If we could make the process faster and cheaper, perhaps drug companies could make the drug available to more people who need it. Some pharma companies are using analytics to speed up the process of bringing a medicine into the hands of those who would benefit.

GlaxoSmithKline (GSK) is a three-hundred-year-old company focused on pharmaceuticals, consumer healthcare, and vaccines. From asthma inhaler Advair, to stomach medicine Tums, to headache medicine Excedrin, to toothpastes Aquafresh and Sensodyne, Nicorette, and Abreva for cold sores, GSK has many products we use every day.

GSK needs to find new ways to bring medicines to the market because the old model is not sustainable. They are using data to help get to the answer faster, enabling scientists to make decisions faster.[19] Mark Ramsay, the R&D Chief Data and Analytics Officer for GSK, spoke with me in a phone interview. Prior to GSK, he served as the Chief Data Officer for Samsung Mobile. Ramsay's team is blending artificial intelligence and machine learning for predictive analytics that can help GSK speed up the research phases of bringing a product to market. For example, his team is using predictive analytics in clinical trials. Using predictive analytics to identify where the clinical trial should be held impacts the entire process and has a big impact on the way the trial is executed and the ability to recruit patients who fit.

Ramsay said, "Historically what a data scientist would do is look at a number of factors and build a model based on a portfolio of factors. Those predictive models would use an algorithm called logistic regression. The factors that influence the outcome you're looking for." Today, machine learning looks at all of the decisions that are being made. Instead of a data scientist looking at predictive factors, it's executed in the machine-learning algorithm. Ramsay says we are just at the beginning of artificial intelligence and machine learning—where the pace of advancement of the algorithms is "astonishing." He said, "Literally things that were impossible to do three years ago are now possible. For example, computer vision and image analytics—that is an extremely difficult problem to solve."

Ramsay, although trained as an engineer, spends time acting as a translator for business problems. Within GSK, his customer tends to be a scientist with a language of their own. The customer Ramsay deals with is technical but in biology or chemistry. He says that a lot of the discussions with his constituents are at the scientific level; they can't understand the technical detail as it relates to the technology so Ramsay and his team broker those exchanges. Increasingly we are seeing a need for technical people to act as translator for a business audience, and vice versa.

Lessons from GSK on Analytics

- Ensure your head of engineering can sit down with the business constituents and understand what they need.
- Use AI machine learning for predictive analytics.
- Enable machine learning to look at all of the decisions that are being made and identify opportunities and patterns.

SOLVING ACROSS THE EXPERIENCE WITH DATA, AI, AND MACHINE LEARNING

Mary Winfield, VP of Customer Experience and Trust at Lyft, describes Lyft as an emotion company. Lyft is an on-demand transportation company based in San Francisco, founded by John Zimmer and Logan Green. The company sees itself as a transportation company focused on delivering exceptional experience, because they believe the experience of the driver and the rider matters above all else. Like many of the other companies listed in this book, Lyft also considers itself a data-driven company, meaning data is used in nearly all decisions made at every level. But what is noteworthy about Lyft is they are not interested in solving for one transactional opportunity, they are looking for opportunities to solve problems across the experience for both rider and driver, both of whom are referred to as customers. Lyft is also using predictive analytics to identify what causes the highest amount of customer pain.

Winfield talks about how she is using a mix of the technology and the human to create a more human experience. For example, if a passenger leaves her smartphone in the back seat, she is going to be in a different emotional state than if she left a sweatshirt. The customer that loses the smartphone wants a person to call her and let her know where the lost item is and when she can expect it back. They are looking at other customer pain points such as if the estimated time of arrival was longer than expected, or if the ride was more expensive than expected. They have built a monitoring system to identify scenarios, with triggers that notify the team. However, not all pain points are equal. Lyft is solving for the more emotional customer pain points with a more white glove approach than the less painful experiences. They are measuring things such as emotional complexity.

Winfield says that the availability of data to make decisions and run the business is a challenge because of the volume of data they have. She explains that when a company is selling a widget or a chatbot the data is generally oriented around the product, and not the customer. "Because we are an experience company, we have data across the experience and we can see what is working and what is not working." The team believes the trick is to look at the customer journey but consider context. With every technology decision made, Lyft is thinking about both driver and rider and asking why.

As a customer, we know what it feels like to have a sequence of communications or events in the experience, but often that experience feels thoughtless and random. The experience is built without the customer in mind, focused on either how to sell the customer more product, or how to solve the problem quickly and cheaply. Lyft is thinking about the evolution of the customer experience, looking at data to figure out the logical first step. The team is continuously coming back to the *why* in the data. Why is the customer using the technology, and what is the customer's story? When it comes to customer experience, Lyft aims to automate some aspects and bring in a person when she feels it's necessary to do so.

Lyft is using predictive analytics in the form of machine learning and artificial intelligence to create a closed-loop feedback cycle with customers and eliminate customer pain. Lyft started out with classification, then moved onto anticipation and quantification of defects. These are signals that help Lyft iterate systemic improvements and enable customer resolution sometimes without or before customers contact them. This is a great example of how a company is using data, AI, and machine learning to decrease the need for the customer to contact the company, solving problems in the background so the customer doesn't even know there was ever a problem. Not only is Lyft using the same AI and machine learning to solve customer problems before they happen, they are contextualizing and personalizing the customer service interactions not by removing humans from the process, but by providing a rich data set of context and information so the human can fully resolve the problem for the customer.

Lessons from Lyft's Use of Predictive Analytics

▸ Think of employees as your first customers.
▸ Consider using predictive analytics in the form of machine learning and artificial intelligence to create a closed-loop feedback cycle with customers and eliminate customer pain.
▸ Solve problems across the experience rather than as one transactional opportunity.
▸ Think about the customer journey, and the relevance of your communications to the customer.
▸ Contextualize and personalize the customer service interaction not by removing humans from the process, but by providing humans a rich data set of context and information so the human can fully resolve the problem for the customer.

Today we have more tools at our fingertips than ever before to gain insights into the customer experience. In this chapter we learned about customer lifetime value and a new way to think about corporate valuation based on new forms of analytics. We looked at predictive, prescriptive, and descriptive analytics and how we can apply them to our businesses to make accurate investments in the customer experience. GSK, Lyft, and Caesars showed us how we can apply different forms of analytics to increase efficiencies, solve for customer problems across the customer journey, and use real-time analytics to make smarter marketing investments.

At this point in the book you have learned about what leading companies are doing to create a customer experience mindset, to create an ideal culture, and to foster leadership development. You have learned about how to create zero-friction customer experiences, customer-focused marketing, and what a customer experience management approach looks like. We've discussed digital transformation and considered how analytics can help our customer focus. Now we will take a look at an important growing field called "data ethics."

10

ETHICS AND DATA PRIVACY IN CUSTOMER EXPERIENCE

> I have as much privacy as a goldfish in a bowl.
> —PRINCESS MARGARET[1]

Go online and you see your friends, family, and coworkers readily sharing personal details and photos of themselves. We gladly gave our data up in the past, not concerned that there would be repercussions. But today there is more awareness about data, and how companies may or may not be ethical with customer data.

When it comes to our data, we are often hands-off about it until something happens. When someone steals our credit card and we get a fraud alert, we feel suddenly vulnerable. Increasingly, brands do not seem in control of customer data. The largest breach of all time was Yahoo! in 2016 with 3 billion accounts compromised. The year 2018 saw 50 million users compromised at Facebook. Marriott had 500 million users' information compromised.[2] Other hacks in 2018 included Quora, British Airways, and Ticketmaster.

Governments have started to get involved, at least in Europe. In May 2018, the General Data Protection Regulation (GDPR) began providing greater transparency into the way that personal data is used. According to the European Commission, personal data is any information "relating to an individual, whether it relates to his or her private, professional or public life. It can be anything from a name, a home address, a photo, an email address, bank details, posts on social networking websites, medical information, or a computer's IP address."[3] As governments become more serious about their role in protecting consumer privacy, and citizens awaken to their own rights, data ethics and privacy will become an important piece of any company's data strategy. Companies can start by taking a stance on the ethical use of data within their own companies, and the behavior they will and won't stand for.

SOCIAL MEDIA, FAKE FOLLOWERS, AND IDENTITY THEFT

You don't worry about your data until the wrong person gets it into their hands. I have had to think about my own data, because I work to build a personal brand online, and I post a lot of content that includes photos and videos. When my daughter was about six months old, I made the decision to stop posting photos of her online, and asked my family to do the same. Not only are hackers gaining access to personal information, but criminals grab images that we innocently post to social media. Social media companies create bots and even steal people's identities online.

In November, Facebook disclosed to investors that it had at least twice as many fake users as it previously estimated, indicating that it has up to 60 million automated accounts. These bots sway advertising audiences and reshape political debates. They can defraud businesses and ruin reputations. Yet their creation and sale fall into a legal gray zone. On Twitter, 48 million active users—about 15 percent—are automated accounts designed to simulate real people, though the company claims that number is far lower. The *New York Times* reported that some companies even steal the identity of real people and create fake accounts with their images in order to generate thousands of followers and retweets, likes, and social media reputation for influencers, actors, athletes, celebrities, and more. Scattered around the web is an array of websites where anonymous bot makers connect with retailers who sell them.[4]

This year my identity was stolen and used to scam people. One day I received a Facebook message from a person who said he had been scammed out of money by a company that advertised me on their website. I typed in the URL and there I was, smiling at my computer, looking eager and ready to serve customers on www.365expertoption.com. They had taken a photo of me working from home at my laptop from Instagram. The website offered trading and bitcoin. It claimed to have four employees, and one of those employees was me, according to the photo on the website. They even used my real name. I was very angry and felt helpless. The company said it was listed in the UK, but was actually based out of India. I was at a loss. I contacted the company through a chat on the website, and the response I got from a person on the other end of the chat was "haha." I contacted them again and again as did my friends. But they were clearly not afraid. Should I get a lawyer? Soon after this discovery, through a quick Facebook search, my husband discovered they had created an entire Facebook profile for me as well. They had created an entire narrative of my life with Instagram, with inspirational quotes next to images I had posted there. The social media account was clearly made to reinforce my identity as an employee on their website. When I reported it to Facebook through an "abuse" button that said "report this profile," I got no response.

It took an employee at Facebook who I knew personally to create a ticket for Facebook to take action and remove the page. I was disappointed by the lack of response from the social media site.

After the Facebook page was taken down, I wanted my photo off the website. I consulted with friends, family, and even my Facebook and LinkedIn networks. Some told me to let it go and there was nothing I could do. Others tried to sell me services. Eventually, my husband's younger brother—who is good with technology—figured out who the website was registered with, and gave me the phone number of the host. The host provider was based in the US, and I was thrilled that in less than a week they took the website down.

I felt validated in my personal digital practice of not posting photos of my daughter online, because now, as I realize, anyone can take anything of yours online, and do what they want with it, and you might never know.

Many people feel out of control about their data. There is no way to keep track of it all. In a recent survey from Pew, only 9 percent of customers say they have control over the data that is collected about them.[5] After this experience, I had a new outlook on data privacy. It is scary what can happen.

One of the highlights of attending the Consumer Electronics Show (CES) in 2019 was a surprise meeting with Tom Wilson, the CEO of Allstate. Although known as an insurance company, Allstate has ventured into other areas, including helping individuals manage their personal digital footprint. Allstate conducted a survey of a thousand people in 2018 to find out how many accounts people thought they had created. The research showed a major gap in how many accounts users assumed they had, and how many they actually had opened. Why is this significant? Every time you have purchased anything, anytime you have signed up for anything on any website, that information has been retained about you. The survey showed 87 percent of people thought they had fifty accounts opened, when it reality they had three times that many. Allstate is in the early phases of a new product called Digital Footprint, which helps users see how many accounts they have opened, where, and allows them to easily delete accounts and manage their information. Wilson showed me his own smartphone, and an image resembling a globe with small dots all over the sphere. The dots represented where he had accounts opened. He told me he personally had four hundred accounts. I imagined that I must have a thousand.

According to Wilson, customer data is the new currency. People care about the safety of their identity but feel there is nothing they can personally do to get a handle on it. Sitting at the CES Allstate booth, discussing privacy, I thought of the thousands of technologies displayed in the exhibit hall. Whether it's a virtual reality headset, or an autonomous car of the future, every company has the customer's data. And we have not seen companies do a great job in recent years of protecting the customer's data from hacks and data breaches. Social networks have also not been transparent about missteps, such as the Cambridge Analytica scandal when the Facebook data of 87 million users was compromised and used for political gain.[6] Most customers have no idea how much data of theirs every single company has. They never read the privacy agreements to find out who has control over their information and what it will be used for. Wilson said in our interview that these are not really privacy agreements, but simply "data access agreements." And often they are not helping customers, who have no clear idea of how the data actually will be used. According to a report from PwC, 63 percent of customers said they would be more open to sharing their data with a company they valued and trusted.

Apple was a company at CES that took a stand on customer data. On the side of a hotel, Apple took out a giant advertisement that said, "What happens on your iPhone stays on your iPhone," a play on the host city's slogan, "What happens in Vegas stays in Vegas."

Apple has always been a proponent of customer privacy. The billboard at CES included the URL for Apple's privacy page, which says, "Apple products are designed to protect your privacy." Apple's stance made headlines a few years ago when the company refused to unlock an iPhone belonging to a suspect in the San Bernardino terrorist attack. Whether morally right or wrong, Apple stood by its privacy policy, refusing to build a back door to the iPhone that Apple said would put all of its customers' privacy at risk. In contrast, Amazon's and Google's devices have been accused of listening to conversations and using that information to sell customers products they've been talking about. However, this accusation has not been verified.

Building trust with customers has never been more important than it is now.

Almost 90 percent of US consumers say that how much they trust a company determines how much they're willing to share personal information.[7]

THE DATA IS NOT THE PROBLEM—IT'S THE PEOPLE WHO USE THE DATA

As we established, customers are willing to trade information and privacy over to organizations that prove they can be trusted with it. As companies build out increasingly advanced data architecture, artificial intelligence, and as robotic process automation makes its way into everyday life, we will need to ensure we are acting ethically. If the past is any indicator of the future, we are facing a crisis of ethics regarding customer data, because companies have not done a great job of protecting it. According to Norm Judah, former Worldwide Services CTO of Microsoft, it's not just that businesses will need to alter their approach to customer data, they will need to create "AI manifestos," an expression of their beliefs and behaviors in the ethical use of data and AI technologies. Judah told me in a video interview that, fueled by vast amounts of data and practically limitless data storage, researchers have been creating breakthrough advances in the field of AI. For example, in the last year, AI systems have achieved human parity in machine comprehension and translation abilities. Judah said that as these breakthroughs continue the future will be different from today, and it's up to each one of us to create the future that we want to see. He believes that while we used to say that every company would become a software company, today not only is every company a software company, but an AI company.

With AI and machine learning, we are teaching computers to do tasks that people once did. With machine learning we are feeding machines large amounts of data so they can learn and identify patterns. However, if the data the machine is fed contains unconscious bias, then the outcome of the machine learning will also contain that bias. For example, a quick Google search of the word "engineer" overwhelmingly shows images of men, while a search of the word "assistant" shows women.[8] Judah says in fields of research, bias and intelligibility will have a large focus. The impact of societal biases reflected in data at scale has become very real to all consumers as they search the internet today. Those search biases potentially impact billions of people every day.

We do not have any kind of framework today for broad commercial adoption of AI, and Judah says that enabling the benefits of AI in applications related to people requires access to great amounts of data about people. If you are empathetic to your customers, you have a customer experience mindset when creating data and AI policies.

FACIAL RECOGNITION AND ETHICS

Facial recognition works by comparing selected facial features from a given image with faces within a database. Many of our personal devices are already using these technologies, quickly identifying which family members are in a photo that you've taken on your phone.

Machines are already learning to read faces, and to interpret expressions as well. Due to advances in the area of neural networks, we have a more accurate facial analysis than we had in the past. Chinese companies recently tested facial recognition software to help police predict crimes before they happened. Additionally, Faception, an Israeli company, sells facial analysis software to governments for security uses. The upside for customer experience is that if we can read customers' faces we can better understand how they're feeling—and that leads to better knowledge about their level of satisfaction with a product or service. However, there are security concerns that must be addressed before the release of these technologies to the broader public.

The technology raises questions of privacy, even when something might seem ethical. For example, take pop icon Taylor Swift, who has hundreds of thousands of fans all over the world. She was the victim of stalking and one man even broke into her New York City apartment and took a shower and a nap in her home. After receiving numerous death threats, Swift took her safety into her own hands. At a Taylor Swift concert at the Rose Bowl, a kiosk was playing rehearsal footage. At the kiosk, concertgoers' faces were scanned in order to be cross-referenced with a Nashville database of the pop star's known stalkers. This is one of those gray areas. Taylor Swift has a database of stalkers, and that is absolutely frightening. But at the same time, these fans did not know their faces were being scanned and that data was collected. Was it ethical for Swift to do this?[9] Private companies don't need consent to do this. There is no government concern, only an ethical one (and a potential business one if it caused a public backlash where people refused to buy Swift's music or attend her concerts).

IOT AND CUSTOMER PRIVACY

IoT is an exciting innovation that promises to benefit society in many ways, but it also presents dangers. By 2020, it's estimated there will be four IoT devices for every person.[10] Smart home products have generated excitement, and make customers lives easier and better; however, we've seen many hacks conducted through IoT devices in businesses and homes. One hacker accessed the data of high rollers in a casino by hacking into the thermostat of the aquarium in the lobby.[11]

A few years ago, a man hacked into a baby monitor in the middle of the night, saw the baby's name on the wall, and started screaming at her.[12] Clearly it is still early days and we have not figured out how to completely secure smart devices. Consumers are nervous about their privacy. In one survey on consumer privacy and IoT, 92 percent said they want to control what personal information is automatically collected. A similar number of respondents want to increase punishments for companies that violate consumers' privacy. These consumers are looking for commitments from government and industry to protect privacy with full disclosure of how the data will be used and shared with third parties.[13] Gartner predicts IoT security spending will hit $1.5 billion by the end of the year, up 28 percent from 2017, and more than double to $3.1 billion by 2021.[14]

Data ethics is not an easy issue. The focus of data management is still a relatively young discipline. Data is today's currency and we are still awkwardly fumbling through this modern era, where the ethical line is not always clear. These issues of ethics and privacy demand thoughtful leaders who understand the issues at hand, and have both employees' and customers' best interests at heart.

CONCLUSION

W hen I set out to write this book, it was going to be about technology. I had a book deal based on the idea of a book on customer experience technology. I spent months meeting with executives, doing research, and even writing part of the book. But when I went to Amazon headquarters, I had an epiphany. I realized that it wasn't the technology that created incredible customer experiences. It was the mindset. It was the attitude of the people who worked there. Most companies simply couldn't get it right, no matter how much they said they wanted to.

The simple act of being customer-focused over being product-focused, and incorporating that customer focus into every single decision and aspect of the business, sounds easy, but in practice it is not easy. Technologies come and go.

It is the culture, the leadership, and the purpose of the organization that matters. But something so seemingly simple is still very hard for most companies.

Companies that created amazing customer experiences did so because they had the intention to. This intention is clear to me no matter if I am talking to the CEO, a recruiter, the Chief Technology Officer, or a customer service representative.

In the beginning of this book, I promised you that becoming a customer-focused organization is not easy and there was no gimmick or shortcut. I hope you have learned that, although it's not easy, it is simple. It is the process of making customer-focused decisions across your organization. Senior executives today can no longer afford to work in an ivory tower. The modern executive must have at least a cursory understanding of the guiding principles I've written about in this book. Modern leaders must work cross-functionally and understand the various aspects of the business, even if they've never needed to know before.

You might realize at this point there is no one definition for customer experience and there is no one-size-fits-all approach. I have given you what I believe makes a customer experience, but there are thousands of other resources out there to help you do so. My goal in writing this book was to equip you with inspiration, ideas, and resources to help make your company more customer-focused.

One of themes in this book is customer experience and how the decisions you make internally impact the customer's experience of your brand externally. Creating internal efficiencies for your employees is an important step for creating better customer experiences. One of the reasons I love the topic of "efficiency" as much as I do is I believe it's important to make life better for people. What makes the human race great is our pursuit of happiness, our commitment to creating a better world. If we can create more efficiencies, life will be less stressful for employees in their jobs, and for customers who would prefer to be with their loved ones rather than stuck in broken products and services.

Experience is the thing that, as human beings, lights our eyes up or makes our blood boil. A positive experience stops us in our tracks and makes us feel good. We know that in our own lives when we make people feel good, they want to be around us, and when we make them feel bad—or make their lives harder—they don't want to be around us anymore. So how can we take this commonsense principle and apply it to our businesses? Making customers feel good requires time, resources, and thought into how we run our companies. It's both the big decisions and the small decisions we make every day. We must start with the intention, adopt the mindset, and be willing to die trying. As we spoke about the blind cave fish at the beginning of this book, today requires a willingness to evolve, and adapt to our new environment.

INTRODUCTION

1. Joshua J. Mark, "Heraclitus of Ephesus," *Ancient History Encyclopedia*, last modified July 14, 2010, https://www.ancient.eu/Heraclitus_of_Ephesos/.
2. Michael Le Page, "Blind Cave Fish Lost Eyes by Unexpected Evolutionary Process," *New Scientist*, last modified October 12, 2017, https://www.newscientist.com/article/2150233-blind-cave-fish-lost-eyes-by-unexpected-evolutionary-process/.
3. "Mexican Tetra," *Wikipedia*, last modified February 15, 2019, https://en.wikipedia.org/wiki/Mexican_tetra.
4. "Black Death," *Wikipedia*, last modified February 26, 2019, https://en.wikipedia.org/wiki/Black_Death.
5. Matt McBride, "Speed, Adaptation and the Pace of Change," *CIO*, last modified September 6, 2018, https://www.cio.com/article/3304276/speed-adaptation-and-the-pace-of-change.html.
6. Ralph Ryback, "Why We Resist Change," *Psychology Today*, last modified January 25, 2017, https://www.psychologytoday.com/us/blog/the-truisms-wellness/201701/why-we-resist-change.
7. Mark J. Perry, "Only 53 US Companies Have Been on the Fortune 500 since 1955, Thanks to the Creative Destruction That Fuels Economic Prosperity," *AEIdeas*, last modified May 23, 2018, https://www.aei.org/publication/only-53-us-companies-have-been-on-the-fortune-500-since-1955-thanks-to-the-creative-destruction-that-fuels-economic-prosperity/.
8. IA Staff, "70% of Buying Experiences Are Based on How the Customer Feels They Are Being Treated," *Industry Analysts*, last modified December 4, 2017, https://industryanalysts.com/12417_greatamerica/.
9. Boundless Psychology, "Biology of Emotion," *Lumen Candela*, accessed March 3, 2019, https://courses.lumenlearning.com/boundless-psychology/chapter/biology-of-emotion/.
10. Psy Blog, "Body Map of Emotions: Happiness Activates the Whole Body," *Spring*, last modified January 2, 2014, https://www.spring.org.uk/2014/01/the-body-map-of-emotions-happiness-activates-the-whole-body.php.
11. "Frustration," *Wikipedia*, last modified February 23, 2019, https://en.wikipedia.org/wiki/Frustration.
12. Temkin Group, "Report: Tech Vendor NPS & Loyalty Benchmark, 2018 (B2B)," *Experience Matters*, last modified September 10, 2018, https://experiencematters.blog/category/temkin-group-research/business-impact/.

13. Kyle O'Brien, "Wunderman Unveils the Concept of 'Wantedness' at Ces," *The Drum,* last modified January 5, 2017, https://www.thedrum.com/news /2017/01/05/wunderman-unveils-the-concept-wantedness-ces.; Charlotte Rogers, "Consumers Will Spend More on Simple Brand Experiences," *Marketing Week,* last modified February 3, 2017, https://www.marketingweek .com/2017/02/03/consumers-spend-more-simple-brand-experiences/.

14. David Clarke and Ron Kinghorn, *Experience Is Everything: Here's How to Get It Right* (New York: PwC, 2018).

CHAPTER 1: CUSTOMER EXPERIENCE MINDSET

1. Chris Lake, "10 Customer Experience Soundbites from Jeff Bezos," *Econsultancy,* last modified August 6, 2013, https://econsultancy.com/10 -customer-experience-soundbites-from-jeff-bezos/.

2. "72% of Businesses Name Improving Customer Experience Their Top Priority," *Forrester,* last modified April 12, 2016, https://go.forrester.com /press-newsroom/72-of-businesses-name-improving-customer-experience -their-top-priority/.

3. Jim Dicso, "Why Personalization Is Key for Retail Customer Experiences," *Retail Customer Experience,* last modified October 19, 2017, https://www .retailcustomerexperience.com/blogs/why-personalization-is-key-for-retail -customer-experiences/.

4. Clarke and Kinghorn, *Experience Is Everything.*

5. Jeremy Finch, "What Is Generation Z, and What Does It Want?" *Fast Company,* last modified April 5, 2015, https://www.fastcompany.com/3045317 /what-is-generation-z-and-what-does-it-want.

6. Finch, "What Is Generation Z, and What Does It Want?"

7. Bulldog Reporter, "How the Experience Economy Is Poised to Skyrocket in 2018," *Agility PR Solutions,* last modified January 9, 2018, https://www .agilitypr.com/pr-news/public-relations/experience-economy-poised -skyrocket-2018/.

8. Eventbrite, "Millennials: Fueling the Experience Economy," *Eventbrite blog,* accessed March 19, 2019, https://www.eventbrite.com/blog/academy /millennials-fueling-experience-economy/.

9. Paul Ratner, "Want Happiness? Buy Experiences, Not Things, Says a Cornell Psychologist," *Big Think,* last modified July 22, 2016, https://bigthink .com/paul-ratner/want-happiness-buy-experiences-not-more-stuff.

10. Pamela N. Danziger, "What the Belmond Acquisition Means for LVMH," *Forbes,* last modified December 16, 2018, https://www.forbes.com/sites /pamdanziger/2018/12/16/what-the-belmond-acquisition-means-for -lmvh/#6fa7c54e7ca1.

11. "Financial Crisis of 2007–2008," *Wikipedia,* last modified March 1, 2019, https://en.wikipedia.org/wiki/Financial_crisis_of_2007%E2%80%932008.

12. "Madoff Investment Scandal," *Wikipedia,* last modified February 1, 2019, https://en.wikipedia.org/wiki/Madoff_investment_scandal; "Ponzi Scheme," *Wikipedia,* last modified March 2, 2019, https://en.wikipedia .org/wiki/Ponzi_scheme.

13. Statista, "Number of Smartphone Users Worldwide from 2014 to 2020 (in Billions)," *Statista,* accessed March 2, 2019, https://www.statista.com /statistics/330695/number-of-smartphone-users-worldwide/.

14. Dan Goldman, "Cashing in on the US Experience Economy," *McKinsey Insights,* last modified December 2017, https://www.mckinsey.com/industries

/private-equity-and-principal-investors/our-insights/cashing-in-on-the-us
-experience-economy.

15. "Host an Experience on Airbnb," *Airbnb*, accessed March 2, 2019, https://
www.airbnb.com/host/experiences.

16. Azadeh Williams, "10 Epic Marketing Campaign Fails Pulled after Public
Backlash," *IDG Communications*, last modified April 13, 2017, https://
www.cmo.com.au/article/617581/10-epic-marketing-fails-pulled-after
-public-backlash/.

17. Microsoft, "2017 State of Global Customer Service Report," *Microsoft
Corporation*, last modified 2017, http://info.microsoft.com/rs/157-GQE
-382/images/EN-CNTNT-Report-DynService-2017-global-state-customer
-service-en-au.pdf.

18. "Customer Expectations Hit All-Time Highs," *Salesforce Blog*, accessed
March 19, 2019, https://www.salesforce.com/research/customer
-expectations/.

19. Alison E. Berman and Jason Dorrier, "Technology Feels Like It's
Accelerating—Because It Actually Is," *Singularity University*, last modified
March 22, 2016, https://singularityhub.com/2016/03/22/technology
-feels-like-its-accelerating-because-it-actually-is/#sm.001gau1b5gx5dtu11
po1aq0yr2flk.

20. "Digital in 2019," *We Are Social*, accessed March 19, 2019, https://weare
social.com/global-digital-report-2019.

21. Clarke and Kinghorn, *Experience Is Everything*.

22. "Facebook, Apple, Amazon, Netflix and Google," *Wikipedia*, last modified
February 9, 2019, https://en.wikipedia.org/wiki/Facebook,_Apple,_
Amazon,_Netflix_and_Google.

23. AWS, "Netflix Case Study," *Amazon*, accessed March 19, 2019, https://aws
.amazon.com/solutions/case-studies/netflix/.

24. Ross Benes, "Better Data Analysis Is Critical to Improving Customer Experience," *eMarketer*, last modified March 16, 2018, https://www.emarketer.com
/content/better-data-analysis-is-critical-to-improving-customer-experience.

25. George Westerman, "Digitally Mature Firms Are 26% More Profitable
Than Their Peers," *MIT Initiative on the Digital Economy*, last modified August 8, 2013, http://ide.mit.edu/news-blog/blog/digitally-mature-firms
-are-26-more-profitable-their-peers.

26. Prachi Bhardwaj, "Amazon Executives Sat through a Brutally Uncomfortable 4.5-Minute Phone Call That Showed Them Just How Much Jeff
Bezos Cares About Customers," *Business Insider*, last modified April 20,
2018, https://www.businessinsider.com/jeff-bezos-amazon-customer-service
-2018-4.

27. "Consumers Connecting with Companies," *Customer Thermometer*, accessed
March 19, 2019, https://www.customerthermometer.com/consumers
-connecting-with-companies/.

28. Belinda Parmar, "The Most Empathetic Companies, 2016," *Harvard Business Review*, last modified December 20, 2016, https://hbr.org/2016/12
/the-most-and-least-empathetic-companies-2016.

29. Kaan Ersun, "Customer Experience Investment: Making the Case on the
ROI of Improved Customer Service," *Solvvy*, last modified March 1, 2018,
https://solvvy.com/blog/customer-experience-investment-making-case
-roi-improved-customer-service/.

30. Lauren Thomas and Courtney Reagan, "Watch out, Retailers. This Is
Just How Big Amazon Is Becoming," *CNBC*, last modified July 13, 2018,

https://www.cnbc.com/2018/07/12/amazon-to-take-almost-50-percent
-of-us-e-commerce-market-by-years-end.html; Kate Taylor, Mary Hanbury, and Dennis Green, "Amazon's Growth Could Threaten These 10
Industries," *Business Insider*, last modified June 28, 2018, https://www
.businessinsider.com/amazon-is-killing-these-7-companies-2017-7#package
-delivery-and-logistics-10.

31. Taylor, Hanbury, and Green, "Amazon's Growth Could Threaten These
    10 Industries."

32. Brad Stone, *Everything Store: Jeff Bezos and the Age of Amazon* (New York:
    Little, Brown and Company, 2013), p. 15.

33. Xueming Luo, Vamsi K. Kanuri, and Michelle Andrews, "Long CEO Ten-
    ure Can Hurt Performance," *Harvard Business Review*, last modified March
    2013, https://hbr.org/2013/03/long-ceo-tenure-can-hurt-performance.

34. Michael Jarret, "Six Reasons CEOs Fail," *INSEAD Knowledge*, last modified
    July 26, 2018, https://knowledge.insead.edu/leadership-organisations
    /six-reasons-ceos-fail-9806.

35. Whitney Hess, "Purpose of a Business Is to Create a Customer," *Whitney
    Georgina Hess Blog*, last modified August 13, 2012, https://whitneyhess
    .com/blog/2012/08/13/the-purpose-of-a-business-is-to-create-a-customer.

36. Rob van der Meulen and Christy Pettey, "Gartner Survey Reveals That
    CEO Priorities Are Shifting to Embrace Digital Business," *Gartner*, last
    modified May 1, 2018, https://www.gartner.com/en/newsroom/press
    -releases/2018-05-01-gartner-survey-reveals-that-ceo-priorities-are-shifting
    -to-embrace-digital-business.

37. van der Meulen and Pettey, "Gartner Survey Reveals That CEO Priorities
    Are Shifting to Embrace Digital Business."

38. Pamela N. Danziger, "Sephora, Ulta and the Battle for the $56B U.S.
    Beauty Retail Market," ibid., last modified August 6, 2018, https://www
    .forbes.com/sites/pamdanziger/2018/08/06/sephora-and-ulta-are-on
    -a-collision-course-then-there-is-amazon-where-is-us-beauty-retail-headed
    /#b8ff7c955dde.

39. Laura M. Holson, "How Sephora Is Thriving Amid a Retail Crisis," *New
    York Times*, last modified May 11, 2017, https://www.nytimes.com/2017
    /05/11/fashion/sephora-beauty-retail-technology.html.

40. Anjali Raguraman, "Rihanna Makes Surprise Appearance at Sephora in
    Singapore for Fenty Beauty Anniversary," *SPH Digital News*, last modified
    October 2, 2018, https://www.straitstimes.com/lifestyle/fashion/rihanna
    -makes-surprise-appearance-at-sephora-in-singapore-for-fenty-beauty.

41. Andrea Park, "Fenty Beauty Is on Its Way to Outselling Both Kylie Cos-
    metics and KKW Beauty *Combined*," *Allure*, last modified January 28, 2018,
    https://www.allure.com/story/fenty-beauty-outselling-kylie-cosmetics
    -kkw-beauty-2018.

42. Rachel Nussbaum, "Sephora Cast Its Own Employees for Its Most Diverse
    Campaign Yet," *Glamour—Condé Nast*, last modified October 30, 2017,
    https://www.glamour.com/story/sephora-holiday-ad-diversity.

43. "Sephora US," *Great Place to Work Institute*, accessed March 2, 2019,
    https://www.greatplacetowork.com/certified-company/1120141.

CHAPTER 2: BUILDING A CUSTOMER-CENTRIC CULTURE

1. "Service Culture: Happy Employees Mean Happy Customers," *FieldAware*, last modified January 4, 2016, https://www.fieldaware.com/blog/posts /service-culture-happy-employees-happy-customers/.

2. Jacob Morgan, "Why the Millions We Spend on Employee Engagement Buy Us So Little," *Harvard Business Review*, last modified March 10, 2017, https://hbr.org/2017/03/why-the-millions-we-spend-on-employee -engagement-buy-us-so-little.

3. Julia Cupman, "Six Steps to B2B Customer Experience Excellence," *B2B International*, last modified April 17, 2017, https://www.b2binternational .com/publications/six-steps-to-b2b-customer-experience-excellence/.

4. Michael Lee Stallard, Jason Pankau, and Katharine P. Stallard, *Connection Culture: The Competitive Advantage of Shared Identity, Empathy, and Understanding at Work* (Alexandria, VA: ATD Press, 2015).

5. Michael Weiss, "Accounting for Corporate Culture," *Robert Half Management Resources*, last modified August 16, 2017, http://rh-us.mediaroom .com/2017-08-16-Accounting-For-Corporate-Culture.

6. Gallup, *State of the American Manager: Analytics and Advice for Leaders* (Washington, D.C.: Gallup, 2015).

7. "Engaged Workplace," *Gallup*, accessed March 2, 2019, https://www.gallup .com/services/190118/engaged-workplace.aspx.

8. Bill Gentry, "Importance of Empathy in the Workplace," *Center for Creative Leadership*, accessed March 8, 2019, https://www.ccl.org/articles/white -papers/empathy-in-the-workplace-a-tool-for-effective-leadership/.

9. Aja Hoggatt, "Black Women Made History at the 2019 Oscars," *Slate Group*, last modified February 24, 2019, https://slate.com/culture/2019 /02/2019-academy-awards-black-women-win-a-record-number-of-oscars -in-a-single-night.html.

10. Vivian Hunt, Dennis Layton, and Sara Prince, "Why Diversity Matters," *McKinsey Insights*, last modified January, 2015, https://www.mckinsey.com /business-functions/organization/our-insights/why-diversity-matters.

11. Jeff Green, Jordyn Holman, and Janet Paskin, "America's C-Suites Keep Getting Whiter (and More Male, Too)," *Bloomberg*, last modified September 21, 2018, https://www.bloomberg.com/news/articles/2018-09-21/america -s-c-suites-keep-getting-whiter-and-more-male-too.

12. Rocío Lorenzo et al., "How Diverse Leadership Teams Boost Innovation," *Boston Consulting Group*, last modified January 23, 2018, https://www.bcg .com/en-us/publications/2018/how-diverse-leadership-teams-boost -innovation.aspx.

13. Libby Kane, "Meet Generation Z, the 'Millennials on Steroids' Who Could Lead the Charge for Change in the US," *Business Insider*, last modified December 4, 2017, https://www.businessinsider.com/generation -z-profile-2017-9#they-most-resemble-millennials-in-all-but-optimism-6.

14. Mark DeWolf, "12 Stats About Working Women," *U.S. Department of Labor Blog*, last modified March 1, 2017, https://blog.dol.gov/2017/03/01/12 -stats-about-working-women.

15. Bridget Brennan, "Top 10 Things Everyone Should Know About Women Consumers," *Bloomberg*, last modified January 11, 2018, https://www .bloomberg.com/diversity-inclusion/blog/top-10-things-everyone-know -women-consumers/.

16. Syeda Asiya Zenab Kazmi, Marja Naarananoja, and Josu Takala, "Diverse Workforce Supported through 'Transformational Leadership' Ensures

Higher Operational Responsiveness," *GSTF International Journal on Business Review (GBR)* 3, no. 3 (2014).

17. Lynda Gratton and Tamara J. Erickson, "Eight Ways to Build Collaborative Teams," *Harvard Business Review*, last modified November, 2007, https://hbr.org/2007/11/eight-ways-to-build-collaborative-teams.

18. Catherine Clifford, "The Brilliant Business Lesson Behind the Emails Jeff Bezos Sends to His Amazon Executives with a Single '?'," *CNBC*, last modified May 7, 2018, https://www.cnbc.com/2018/05/07/why-jeff -bezos-still-reads-the-emails-amazon-customers-send-him.html.

19. Harry Rollason, "The 10 Most Social Media Minded CEOs," *Conversocial*, last modified February 10, 2017, https://www.conversocial.com/blog /the-10-most-social-media-minded-ceos.

20. Rollason, "The 10 Most Social Media Minded CEOs."

21. Marco Nink and Jennifer Robison, "Damage Inflicted by Poor Managers," *Gallup*, last modified December 10, 2016, https://news.gallup .com/businessjournal/200108/damage-inflicted-poor-managers.aspx.

22. Emma Seppälä, "What Bosses Gain by Being Vulnerable," *Harvard Business Review*, last modified December 11, 2014, https://hbr.org/2014/12 /what-bosses-gain-by-being-vulnerable.

23. Roger Trapp, "Why Successful Leaders Acknowledge Cultural Differences," *Forbes*, last modified June 30, 2014, https://www.forbes.com/sites /rogertrapp/2014/06/30/why-successful-leaders-acknowledge-cultural -differences/#51eaf7f2661f.

24. University of California—Riverside, "Increasing Productivity by One Day Each Month: Study Shows Corporate Wellness Programs Lead to Increased Worker Productivity," *Science Daily*, last modified August 2, 2017, https://www.sciencedaily.com/releases/2017/08/170802134738.htm.

25. Punam Anand Keller, Donald R. Lehmann, and Katherine J. Milligan, "Effectiveness of Corporate Well-Being Programs: A Meta-Analysis," *Journal of Macromarketing* 29, no. 3 (2009).

26. Dimple Agarwal et al., "Well-Being: A Strategy and a Responsibility," *Deloitte Insights*, last modified March 28, 2018, https://www2.deloitte.com /insights/us/en/focus/human-capital-trends/2018/employee-well-being -programs.html.

27. Economic Innovation Group and Ernst & Young, "Millennial Economy: Findings from a New EY & EIG National Survey of Millennials," *EIG*, accessed March 8, 2019, https://eig.org/millennial.

28. Camille Peri, "10 Things to Hate About Sleep Loss," *WebMD*, last modified June 26, 2016, https://www.webmd.com/sleep-disorders/features /10-results-sleep-loss#1.

29. "Udemy in Depth: 2018 Workplace Distraction Report," *Udemy*, accessed March 8, 2019, https://research.udemy.com/research_report/udemy -depth-2018-workplace-distraction-report/.

30. Ryan Browne, "70% of People Globally Work Remotely at Least Once a Week, Study Says," *CNBC*, last modified May 30, 2018, https://www.cnbc .com/2018/05/30/70-percent-of-people-globally-work-remotely-at-least -once-a-week-iwg-study.html.

31. Michelle Robertson, "Stunning Increase in Bay Area 'Super Commuters' in the Last Decade Amid Housing Crisis," *SF Gate*, last modified April 27, 2018, https://www.sfgate.com/traffic/article/Bay-Area-commute-San -Francisco-traffic-12861808.php.

32. "How Corporate Culture Affects the Bottom Line," *Duke University's Fuqua School of Business,* last modified November 12, 2015, https://www.fuqua.duke.edu/duke-fuqua-insights/corporate-culture.

33. "Capital One," *Wikipedia,* last modified February 2, 2019, https://en.wikipedia.org/wiki/Capital_One.

34. Peter High, "How Capital One Became a Leading Digital Bank," *Forbes,* last modified December 12, 2016, https://www.forbes.com/sites/peterhigh/2016/12/12/how-capital-one-became-a-leading-digital-bank/#77a068d215ee.

35. Rachel Gillett, "13 Top Executives Who Have a Salary of $1 or Less," *Inc. Magazine,* last modified August 17, 2015, https://www.inc.com/business-insider/12-top-executives-who-make-one-dollar-or-less.html.

36. "Capital One Financial Corporation," *Great Place to Work Institute,* accessed March 2, 2019, https://www.greatplacetowork.com/certified-company/1000049.

37. "We Choose to Go to the Moon," *Wikipedia,* last modified February 27, 2019, https://en.wikipedia.org/wiki/We_choose_to_go_to_the_Moon.

CHAPTER 3: DEVELOPING CUSTOMER-FOCUSED LEADERSHIP

1. Laura Berlinsky-Schine, "Inspiring Leadership Quotes: 51 Famous Quotes on Women's Leadership," *fairygodboss,* accessed April 15, 2019, https://fairygodboss.com/articles/inspiring-leadership-quotes.

2. Josh Bersin, "It's Not the CEO, It's the Leadership Strategy That Matters," *Forbes,* last modified July 30, 2012, https://www.forbes.com/sites/joshbersin/2012/07/30/its-not-the-ceo-its-the-leadership-strategy-that-matters/#8e89a7a6db86.

3. Stallard, Pankau, and Stallard, *Connection Culture.*

4. Michael Lee Stallard and Jason Pankau, "What U2 and the US Navy Have in Common: Connecting with Core Employees," *Michael Lee Stallard,* last modified June 23, 2010, http://www.michaelleestallard.com/what-u2-and-the-us-navy-have-in-common-connecting-with-core-employees.

5. "Broaden-and-Build," *Wikipedia,* last modified January 26, 2019, https://en.wikipedia.org/wiki/Broaden-and-build#cite_note-1.

6. "2014 Success Achiever of the Year: Reed Hastings," *SUCCESS Magazine,* last modified February 10, 2015, https://www.success.com/2014-success-achiever-of-the-year-reed-hastings/.

7. Blake Morgan, "10 Major Corporate Blunders That Wouldn't Have Happened if Companies Listened to Their Employees," *Forbes,* last modified January 3, 2018, https://www.forbes.com/sites/blakemorgan/2018/01/03/10-major-corporate-blunders-that-wouldnt-have-happened-if-companies-listened-to-their-employees/#1bfeb65343fa.

8. Raj Bharti, "Learn from Amazon's Leadership Principles," *Wharton Magazine,* last modified January 9, 2015, http://whartonmagazine.com/blogs/learn-from-amazons-leadership-principles/#sthash.AxubDJ4v.dpbs.

9. Andy Micone, "What Kind of Companies Employ a Futurist? What's a Best Example of Such Work?" *Quora,* last modified July 28, 2016, https://www.quora.com/What-kind-of-companies-employ-a-futurist-Whats-a-best-example-of-such-work.

10. Ed Catmull and Amy Wallace, *Creativity, Inc.: Overcoming the Unseen Forces That Stand in the Way of True Inspiration* (New York: Random House, 2014).

11. "World's Most Innovative Companies," *Forbes*, accessed March 2, 2019, https://www.forbes.com/innovative-companies/#61f0d9401d65.

CHAPTER 4: DESIGNING THE ZERO-FRICTION CUSTOMER EXPERIENCE

1. "World According to Coco Chanel," *Harper's Bazaar*, last modified August 12, 2017, https://www.harpersbazaar.com/uk/fashion/fashion-news/news/a31524/the-world-according-to-coco-chanel/.
2. Omar Abbosh, "Disruption Need Not Be an Enigma," *Accenture Digital*, last modified February 26, 2018, https://www.accenture.com/us-en/insight-leading-new-disruptability-index.
3. "Six Sigma," *Wikipedia*, last modified March 4, 2019, https://en.wikipedia.org/wiki/Six_Sigma.
4. "W. Edwards Deming," *Wikipedia*, last modified February 15, 2019, https://en.wikipedia.org/wiki/W._Edwards_Deming.
5. Hayley Peterson, "Target's CEO Is Visiting Customers' Homes to Succeed Where Walmart Failed," *Business Insider*, last modified January 21, 2016, https://www.businessinsider.com/targets-ceo-visiting-customer-homes-2016-1.
6. CEO Survey, "CEOs' Curbed Confidence Spells Caution," *PwC*, last modified February 27, 2019, https://www.pwc.com/gx/en/ceo-survey/2019/report/pwc-22nd-annual-global-ceo-survey.pdf.
7. Leonardo Worldwide, "Explosive Growth of Airbnb – an Infographic for Hoteliers," *Vizlly*, accessed March 15, 2019, https://www.vizlly.com/blog-airbnb-infographic/.
8. Julian Close, "Five Stocks with Explosive Growth," *Investors Observer*, last modified June 4, 2018, https://www.investorsobserver.com/market-intelligence-center/editors-picks/five-stocks-with-explosive-growth/.
9. Liz Welch, "How Casper Became a $100 Million Company in Less Than Two Years," *Inc. Magazine*, last modified March 2016, https://www.inc.com/magazine/201603/liz-welch/casper-changing-mattress-industry.html.
10. "Efficiency," *Dictionary.com*, accessed March 15, 2019, https://www.dictionary.com/browse/efficiency.
11. Lynn Kesterson-Townes, "5 Ways Cloud Drives Enterprise Innovation," *IBM*, last modified May 17, 2017, https://www.ibm.com/blogs/cloud-computing/2017/05/17/cloud-drives-enterprise-innovation/.
12. Michael Redbord, "The Hard Truth About Acquisition Costs (and How Your Customers Can Save You)," *HubSpot*, last modified May 9, 2018, https://blog.hubspot.com/news-trends/customer-acquisition-study.
13. Oracle, "Seventy-Seven Percent of Consumers Feel Inefficient Customer Service Experiences Detract from Their Quality of Life," *PR Newswire*, last modified April 10, 2018, https://www.prnewswire.com/news-releases/seventy-seven-percent-of-consumers-feel-inefficient-customer-service-experiences-detract-from-their-quality-of-life-300626778.html.
14. Vanessa McMains and Nelson Lauren, "Study Suggests Medical Errors Now Third Leading Cause of Death in the U.S.," *Johns Hopkins Hospital*, last modified May 3, 2016, https://www.hopkinsmedicine.org/news/media/releases/study_suggests_medical_errors_now_third_leading_cause_of_death_in_the_us.
15. Jeff Lagasse, "Consumer Demand for a Better Patient Experience Fueling Tech Startups," *Healthcare Information and Management Systems Society*,

last modified July 11, 2018, https://www.healthcareitnews.com/news
/consumer-demand-better-patient-experience-fueling-tech-startups.

16. Solutionreach, "The Patient-Provider Relationship Study: The Ripple Effect
Starts with Boomers," *Solutionreach*, last modified June 16, 2017, https://
www.solutionreach.com/rethinking-the-patient-provider-relationship.

17. Lisa Rapaport, "Patients More Satisfied When Doctors Treat Fewer
People," *Reuters*, last modified April 13, 2019, https://www.reuters.com
/article/us-health-patients-physician-reviews/patients-more-satisfied-when
-doctors-treat-fewer-people-idUSKBN1HK2BI.

18. Stephanie Allen, "2019 Global Health Care Outlook: Shaping the Future,"
Deloitte, accessed March 15, 2019, https://www2.deloitte.com/global/en
/pages/life-sciences-and-healthcare/articles/global-health-care-sector
-outlook.html.

CHAPTER 5: CUSTOMER-FOCUSED MARKETING

1. Margaret Dawson, "What I Learned from B2b Content Marketing Expert
Ann Handley," *Rival IQ,* last modified October 3, 2014, https://www
.rivaliq.com/blog/b2b-content-marketing-tips/.

2. Jeff Fromm, "How Much Financial Influence Does Gen Z Have?," *Forbes*,
last modified January 10, 2018, https://www.forbes.com/sites/jefffromm
/2018/01/10/what-you-need-to-know-about-the-financial-impact-of-gen-z
-influence/#66e514256fc5.

3. CMO Council, "CMO Shift to Gaining Business Lift," *Deloitte Development*,
last modified December, 2016, https://cmo.deloitte.com/content/dam
/assets/cmo/Documents/CMO/us-cmo-the-cmo-shift-to-gaining-business
-lift.pdf.

4. CMO Council, "CMO Shift to Gaining Business Lift."

5. "CMO Survey: Marketers Predict More Online Data Use, Less from
Third Parties," *Duke University's Fuqua School of Business*, last modified
August 28, 2018, https://www.fuqua.duke.edu/duke-fuqua-insights
/cmo-survey-aug-2018.

6. Devon McGinnis, "Need-to-Know Marketing Statistics for 2019," *Sales Force
Blog*, last modified January 23, 2019, https://www.salesforce.com/blog
/2019/01/marketing-statistics-to-know.html.

7. Curtis N. Bingham, "The CCO Council 2014 Chief Customer Officer
Study," *Predictive Consulting Group,* last modified 2014, http://www
.ccocouncil.org/site/cco-study.aspx.

8. Matt Ariker et al., "How Marketers Can Personalize at Scale," *Harvard
Business Review*, last modified November 23, 2015, https://hbr.org
/2015/11/how-marketers-can-personalize-at-scale.

9. "New Epsilon Research Indicates 80% of Consumers Are More Likely to
Make a Purchase When Brands Offer Personalized Experiences," *Epsilon
Data Management*, last modified January 9, 2018, https://us.epsilon.com
/pressroom/new-epsilon-research-indicates-80-of-consumers-are-more
-likely-to-make-a-purchase-when-brands-offer-personalized-experiences.

10. Econsultancy, "Digital Intelligence Briefing: 2018 Digital Trends," *Adobe*,
last modified February 2018, https://www.adobe.com/uk/modal-offers
/econsultancy_digital_trends_2018_report.html.

11. "AI-Ready or Not: Artificial Intelligence Here We Come!" *Weber Shand-
wick*, last modified October 19, 2016, https://www.webershandwick.com
/news/ai-ready-or-not-artificial-intelligence-here-we-come/.

12. Braveen Kumar, "User-Generated Content: How to Rally Customers to Create Content with You," *Shopify Blogs*, last modified April 26, 2018, https://www.shopify.com/blog/user-generated-content.

13. Irvine Stewart, "90% of Shoppers' Purchasing Decisions Are Influenced by User-Generated Content," *Medium*, last modified July 27, 2017, https://medium.com/@stewartirvine/90-of-shoppers-purchasing-decisions-are-influenced-by-user-generated-content-64b03abf41c9.

14. Jessica Williams, "User Generated Content Marketing Campaigns: Best Examples from 2018 (So Far…)," *Wayin*, last modified December 18, 2018, https://www.wayin.com/blog/user-generated-content-campaigns-2018/.

15. Danielle Hayes, "11 Smart Examples of UGC Campaigns (Big Brands)," *The Shelf*, last modified August 20, 2018, https://www.theshelf.com/the-blog/user-generated-content-examples.

16. Mindi Chahal, "Why Marketers Are Failing to Target Consumers at Key Life Events," *Marketing Week*, last modified March 4, 2016, https://www.marketingweek.com/2016/03/04/why-marketers-are-failing-to-target-consumers-at-key-life-events/.

17. "US Asks Judge to Give Final Approval to Settlement with CVS to Buy Aetna," *CNBC*, last modified February 26, 2019, https://www.cnbc.com/2019/02/26/us-asks-judge-to-give-final-approval-to-settlement-with-cvs-to-buy-aetna.html.

18. Samuel Stebbins, "The 10 Biggest Mergers and Acquisitions of 2018," *USA Today*, last modified December 10, 2018, https://www.usatoday.com/story/money/business/2018/12/10/mergers-and-acquisitions-2018-10-biggest-corporate-consolidations/38666639/.

19. Molly Fleming, "How Getting Rid of the CMO 'Broadened' Coca-Cola's Marketing Approach," *Marketing Week*, last modified November 14, 2018, https://www.marketingweek.com/2018/11/14/coca-cola-chief-growth-officer/.

20. Jenny Rooney, "CMO Next 2018: The Full List of 50 Chief Marketers," *Forbes*, last modified September 24, 2018, https://www.forbes.com/sites/jenniferrooney/2018/09/24/cmo-next-2018-the-full-list-of-50-chief-marketers/#6154e72b56a3.

21. Thomas Husson, "CMOs: To Get a Seat at the Digital Transformation Table, Command Your Customer's Experience," *Forrester*, last modified February 5, 2019, https://go.forrester.com/blogs/cmos-to-get-a-seat-at-the-digital-transformation-table-command-your-customers-experience/.

22. "Gen Z CSR Study: How to Speak Z," *Cone Communications*, last modified September 13, 2017, http://www.conecomm.com/2017-cone-gen-z-csr-study-pdf.

23. Michael Bush, "2019 Edelman Trust Barometer Reveals 'My Employer' Is the Most Trusted Institution," *PR Newswire*, last modified January 20, 2019, https://www.prnewswire.com/news-releases/2019-edelman-trust-barometer-reveals-my-employer-is-the-most-trusted-institution-300781253.html.

24. Brian Gregg et al., "Marketing's Holy Grail: Digital Personalization at Scale," *McKinsey Insights*, last modified November 2016, https://www.mckinsey.com/business-functions/digital-mckinsey/our-insights/marketings-holy-grail-digital-personalization-at-scalev.

25. "The 2017 State of Personalization Report," *Segment*, last modified October 2017, http://grow.segment.com/Segment-2017-Personalization-Report.pdf.

26. Bernard Marr, "How Harley Davidson Is Using AI and Robots to Prepare for the 4th Industrial Revolution," *Forbes*, last modified July 3, 2018,

https://www.forbes.com/sites/bernardmarr/2018/07/03/how-harley
-davidson-is-using-ai-and-robots-to-prepare-for-the-4th-industrial-revolution
/#517925605271.

27. Marcell Gogan, "How Leading Companies Use AI for Customer Retention," *TechSpective*, last modified May 16, 2018, https://techspective.net
/2018/05/16/how-leading-companies-use-ai-for-customer-retention/.

28. "Spotify," *Wikipedia*, last modified March 15, 2019, https://en.wikipedia
.org/wiki/Spotify.

29. Daniel Newman, "Improving Customer Experience through Customer
Data," *Forbes*, last modified April 4, 2017, https://www.forbes.com/sites
/danielnewman/2017/04/04/improving-customer-experience-through
-customer-data/#9fca5bb4e64d.

30. Josh Ong, "What Tesla's Valuation Says About the Power of Branding,"
Forbes, last modified November 17, 2017, https://www.forbes.com/sites
/forbescommunicationscouncil/2017/11/17/what-teslas-valuation-says
-about-the-power-of-branding/#7c10c82fa65e.

31. Alex Obenauer, "7 Lessons You Can Learn from Tesla About Product Design," *Medium*, last modified September 15, 2016, https://medium.com
/newindustrialist/7-lessons-you-can-learn-from-tesla-about-product-design
-82dc81e639a2.

32. Enrique Dans, "Guess What? Everyone Was Wrong About Tesla," *Forbes*, last
modified October 28, 2018, https://www.forbes.com/sites/enriquedans
/2018/10/28/guess-what-everyone-was-wrong-about-tesla/#4f8f315e3ca4.

33. Neil Strauss, "Elon Musk: The Architect of Tomorrow," *Rolling Stone*, last
modified November 15, 2017, https://www.rollingstone.com/culture
/culture-features/elon-musk-the-architect-of-tomorrow-120850/.

34. Phil LeBeau, "Tesla CEO Elon Musk's Influence Grows as Automakers
Roll out Electric-Vehicle Plans at Detroit Auto Show," *CNBC*, last modified
January 16, 2019, https://www.cnbc.com/2019/01/15/teslas-influence
-grows-as-automakers-charge-up-electric-vehicle-plans.html.

35. Taylor Hatmaker, "Tesla Will End Its Buyer Referral Program for 'Adding
Too Much Cost'," *TechCrunch*, last modified January 2019, https://tech
crunch.com/2019/01/17/tesla-referral-program-end-date/.

36. "Omron," *Wikipedia*, last modified December 23, 2018, https://en.wikipedia
.org/wiki/Omron.

CHAPTER 6: CUSTOMER EXPERIENCE TECHNOLOGY

1. Henry A. Kissinger, "How the Enlightenment Ends," *The Atlantic*, last modified June 2018, https://www.theatlantic.com/magazine/archive/2018/06
/henry-kissinger-ai-could-mean-the-end-of-human-history/559124/.

2. "Customer Experience Management Market Worth 16.91 Billion Usd
by 2022," *Markets and Markets Research*, last modified November 2017,
https://www.marketsandmarkets.com/PressReleases/customer
-experience-management.asp.

3. Nick Ismail, "All Hands on Tech: The Impact of Outdated Technology,"
Information Age, last modified October 26, 2016, https://www.information
-age.com/hands-tech-impact-outdated-technology-123462887/.

4. Tom Starner, "Outdated Tech May Be Costing US Employers $1.8t
Thanks to 'Repetitive Tasks'," *Industry Dive*, last modified March 2, 2016,
https://www.hrdive.com/news/outdated-tech-may-be-costing-us-employers
-18t-thanks-to-repetitive-tasks/414819/.

5. "Employee Engagement Benchmark Study, 2017," *Temkin Group*, last modified March 2017, https://temkingroup.com/product/employee -engagement-benchmark-study-2017/.

6. "2019 State of IT: The Annual Report on IT Budgets and Tech Trends," *Spiceworks*, accessed March 15, 2019, https://www.spiceworks.com /marketing/state-of-it/report/.

7. Patricia Stichnoth, "Everywhere You Look: Computer Vision at Wayfair," *Wayfair Tech Blog*, last modified June 8, 2018, https://tech.wayfair.com /2018/06/everywhere-you-look-computer-vision-at-wayfair/.

8. "How to Think About Data in 2019," *Economist*, last modified December 22, 2018, https://www.economist.com/leaders/2018/12/22/how-to -think-about-data-in-2019.

9. Heather Pemberton Levy, "Gartner Predicts a Virtual World of Exponential Change," *Gartner*, last modified October 18, 2016, https://www .gartner.com/smarterwithgartner/gartner-predicts-a-virtual-world-of -exponential-change/.

10. Clarke and Kinghorn, *Experience Is Everything*.

11. "The Difference between AI, Machine Learning, and Robotics," *Dell Technologies*, accessed March 15, 2019, https://www.delltechnologies.com /en-us/perspectives/the-difference-between-ai-machine-learning-and -robotics.

12. Gil Press, "Forrester Predicts Investment in Artificial Intelligence Will Grow 300% in 2017," *Forbes*, last modified November 1, 2016, https:// www.forbes.com/sites/gilpress/2016/11/01/forrester-predicts-investment -in-artificial-intelligence-will-grow-300-in-2017/#338887de5509.

13. Mary C. Lacity and Leslie Willcocks, "What Knowledge Workers Stand to Gain from Automation," *Harvard Business Review*, last modified June 15, 2015, https://hbr.org/2015/06/what-knowledge-workers-stand-to-gain -from-automation.

14. Amanda Zantal-Wiener, "The State of Voice: Looking Ahead to 2019," *HubSpot*, last modified December 13, 2018, https://blog.hubspot.com /news-trends/the-state-of-voice-2018-2019.

15. Bret Kinsella and Ava Mutchler, "In-Car Voice Assistant Consumer Adoption Report 2019," *Voice Bot*, last modified January 2019, https://voicebot .ai/in-car-voice-assistant-consumer-adoption-report-2019/.

16. Daniel Faggella, "Artificial Intelligence Plus the Internet of Things (IoT)—3 Examples Worth Learning From," *Emerj Artificial Intelligence Research*, last modified February 18, 2019, https://www.techemergence .com/artificial-intelligence-plus-the-internet-of-things-iot-3-examples-worth -learning-from/.

17. Teena Maddox, "Smart Cities: A Cheat Sheet," *Tech Republic*, last modified July 16, 2018, https://www.techrepublic.com/article/smart-cities-the-smart -persons-guide/.

18. "Connected Car and IoT Automotive Cloud Services," *KaaIoT Technologies*, accessed March 15, 2019, https://www.kaaproject.org/automotive.

19. Bernard Marr, "The Amazing Ways Carnival Cruises Is Using IoT and AI to Create Smart Cities at Sea," *Forbes*, last modified March 22, 2019, https://www.forbes.com/sites/bernardmarr/2019/03/22/the-amazing -ways-carnival-cruises-is-using-iot-and-ai-to-create-smart-cities-at-sea/#4398 c6115a64.

20. Shital Chheda, Ewan Duncan, and Stefan Roggenhofer, "Putting Customer Experience at the Heart of Next-Generation Operating Models,"

McKinsey Insights, last modified March 2017, https://www.mckinsey.com /business-functions/digital-mckinsey/our-insights/putting-customer -experience-at-the-heart-of-next-generation-operating-models.

21. Paul-Louis Caylar and Alexandre Ménard, "How Telecom Companies Can Win in the Digital Revolution," ibid., last modified October 2016, https:// www.mckinsey.com/business-functions/digital-mckinsey/our-insights /how-telecom-companies-can-win-in-the-digital-revolution.

22. Gartner, "Every Organizational Function Needs to Work on Digital Transformation," *Harvard Business Review*, last modified November 27, 2018, https://hbr.org/sponsored/2018/11/every-organizational-function-needs -to-work-on-digital-transformation.

23. Jacques Bughin et al., "Digital Europe: Realizing the Continent's Potential," *McKinsey Insights*, last modified June 2016, https://www.mckinsey .com/business-functions/digital-mckinsey/our-insights/digital-europe -realizing-the-continents-potential.

24. "What Does a 'Cloud' Data Center Look Like?" *IDEA*, last modified August 1, 2011, http://www.idea.org/blog/2011/07/28/what-does-a-cloud -data-center-look-like/.

25. "Cloud Computing," *Wikipedia*, last modified March 10, 2019, https://en .wikipedia.org/wiki/Cloud_computing.

26. "What Does a 'Cloud' Data Center Look Like?"

27. "Gartner Forecasts Worldwide Public Cloud Revenue to Grow 17.3 Percent in 2019," *Gartner*, last modified September 12, 2018, https://www .gartner.com/en/newsroom/press-releases/2018-09-12-gartner-forecasts -worldwide-public-cloud-revenue-to-grow-17-percent-in-2019.

28. Laura Wood, "Cloud-Based Contact Center Market—Global Forecast to 2022," *PR Newswire*, last modified April 19, 2018, https://www.prnewswire .com/news-releases/cloud-based-contact-center-market—global-forecast -to-2022-300632955.html.

29. "2018 Cloud Computing Research [Executive Summary]," *IDG Communications*, last modified August 2018, https://resources.idg.com/download /executive-summary/cloud-computing-2018.

30. Ari Levy and Jordan Novet, "Salesforce Is Not the Fastest-Growing Enterprise Software Company Ever—It's Amazon," *CNBC*, last modified December 1, 2018, https://www.cnbc.com/2018/12/01/amazon-web -services-is-growing-faster-than-salesforce.html.

CHAPTER 7: DIGITAL TRANSFORMATION

1. "Lao Tzu Quotes," *BrainyQuote*, accessed April 15, 2019 https://www .brainyquote.com/quotes/lao_tzu_121075.

2. Abbosh, "Disruption Need Not Be an Enigma."

3. Gartner, "Every Organizational Function Needs to Work."

4. Rob Petersen, "11 Inspiring Case Studies of Digital Transformation," *Biznology*, last modified December 28, 2016, https://biznology.com/2016 /12/11-inspiring-case-studies-digital-transformation/.

5. Gartner, "Every Organizational Function Needs to Work."

6. Clint Boulton, "'Digital Laggards' Must Harness Data or Get Left Behind," *CIO*, last modified September 21, 2016, https://www.cio.com/article/3122806 /it-industry/digital-laggards-must-harness-data-or-get-left-behind.html.

7. Megan Burns, Michael E. Gazala, and Carla O'Connor, "The US Customer Experience Index, Q1 2015," *Forrester*, last modified April 20, 2015, https://

www.forrester.com/report/The+US+Customer+Experience+Index+Q1
+2015/-/E-RES117482.

8. Megan Burns, Michael E. Gazala, and Carla O'Connor, "The US Customer
    Experience Index, Q1 2015."

9. Blake Lindsay, Eugéne Smit, and Nick Waugh, "How the Implementation
    of Organizational Change Is Evolving," *McKinsey Insights*, last modified
    February 2018, https://www.mckinsey.com/business-functions/mckinsey
    -implementation/our-insights/how-the-implementation-of-organizational
    -change-is-evolving.

10. Chad Brooks, "Change in the Workplace Stresses Your Employees Out
    Most," *Business News Daily*, last modified May 25, 2017, https://www
    .businessnewsdaily.com/8744-changes-at-work-stress.html.

11. Marshall Cooper, "5 Reasons Why Your Tech Company Should Target
    Sales to CEOs," *Chief Executive Group*, last modified May 26, 2017, https://
    chiefexecutive.net/5-reasons-tech-company-target-sales-ceos/.

12. William Decherd et al., "The Difference between Good and Bad Sales
    Training: A Closer Look at Certification," *McKinsey Insights*, last modi-
    fied February 2019, https://www.mckinsey.com/business-functions
    /marketing-and-sales/our-insights/the-difference-between-good-and-bad
    -sales-training.

13. Unisys, "The New Digital Workplace Divide: U.S. Workers Whose Employer
    Provides Outdated Technology Feel Less Productive, Are 750 Percent
    More Likely to Be Frustrated and 450 Percent More Likely to Want to
    Quit," *PR Newswire*, last modified June 26, 2018, https://www.prnewswire
    .com/news-releases/the-new-digital-workplace-divide-us-workers-whose
    -employer-provides-outdated-technology-feel-less-productive-are-750-percent
    -more-likely-to-be-frustrated-and-450-percent-more-likely-to-want-to-quit
    -300671979.html.

14. Krista Garcia, "Customer Experience Matters to Supply Chain Execs
    Too," *eMarketer*, last modified August 21, 2018, https://www.emarketer
    .com/content/customer-experience-matters-to-supply-chain-execs-too.

15. Lindsey Finch, "Managing the Customer Trust Crisis: New Research
    Insights," *Sales Force Blog*, last modified September 6, 2018, https://
    www.salesforce.com/blog/2018/09/trends-customer-trust-research
    -transparency.html.

16. Eileen Brown, "Gen Z Willing to Provide Their Personal Data for More
    Personalized Experiences," *ZD Net*, last modified March 6, 2019, https://
    www.zdnet.com/article/gen-z-willing-to-provide-their-personal-data
    -for-more-personalized-experiences/.

17. Louis Columbus, "The State of Digital Business Transformation, 2018,"
    Forbes, last modified April 22, 2018, https://www.forbes.com/sites
    /louiscolumbus/2018/04/22/the-state-of-digital-business-transformation
    -2018/#fb8ac6658837.

18. David Trainer and Great Speculation, "Best Buy Rising from Ashes to
    Lead New Retail Paradigm," *Forbes*, last modified June 7, https://www
    .forbes.com/sites/greatspeculations/2018/06/07/best-buy-rising-from
    -ashes-to-lead-new-retail-paradigm/#131ff472b443.

19. Hoang Nguyen, "Target Is America's Most Popular Department Store,"
    YouGov, last modified May 14, 2018, https://today.yougov.com/topics
    /lifestyle/articles-reports/2018/05/14/target-americas-most-popular
    -department-store.

20. Digital Innovation and Transformation, "Target Transforms for the Digital Age," *Harvard Business School,* last modified April 30, 2018, https://digit.hbs.org/submission/target-transforms-for-the-digital-age/#_edn2.

21. Phil Wahba, "How Target Keeps Its 'Tar-Zhay' Luster," *Fortune,* last modified August 22, 2018, http://fortune.com/2018/08/22/target-private -label.

22. Zeeshan Ahmad, "Target Plays to Strength, Combining Digital Sales and Stores," *STL News,* last modified January 10, 2019, https://www.stl .news/new-york-target-plays-to-strength-combining-digital-sales-and-stores /242201/.

23. Veronica Sonosev, "How Sephora Makes Beauty a Two-Way Conversation," *Forbes,* last modified April 12, 2018, https://www.forbes.com/sites /veronikasonsev/2018/04/12/how-sephora-makes-beauty-a-two-way -conversation/#4ae36a5b7f51.

24. Brian Honigman, "How Sephora Integrates Retail & Digital Marketing Strategy," *eTail,* last modified June 27, 2018, https://etailwest.wbresearch .com/how-sephora-integrates-retail-online-marketing.

25. Holson, "How Sephora Is Thriving."

26. Newman, "Improving Customer Experience."

27. Motley Fool Transcribers, "1-800-Flowers.com Inc (FLWS) Q2 2019 Earnings Conference Call Transcript," *Motley Fool,* last modified January 31, 2019, https://www.fool.com/earnings/call-transcripts/2019/01/31/1 -800-flowerscom-inc-flws-q2-2019-earnings-confere.aspx.

28. Lexi Monaghan, "How to Become an Experience-Led Business," *Adobe Blog,* last modified March 24, 2017, https://theblog.adobe.com/become -experience-led-business/.

29. Shelley Cernel, "Selling to the Modern B2B Buyer," *Sales Force Blog,* last modified June 16, 2016, https://www.salesforce.com/blog/2016/06/selling -to-the-modern-b2b-buyer.

30. Cupman, "Six Steps to B2B Customer Experience Excellence."

31. Nicholas Toman, Brent Adamson, and Cristina Gomez, "The New Sales Imperative," *Harvard Business Review,* last modified March–April 2017, https://hbr.org/2017/03/the-new-sales-imperative.

32. Toman, Adamson, and Gomez, "The New Sales Imperative."

33. Eric Almquist, Jamie Cleghorn, and Lori Sherer, "The B2B Elements of Value," *Harvard Business Review,* last modified 2018, https://hbr.org/2018 /03/the-b2b-elements-of-value.

34. Cernel, "Selling to the Modern B2B Buyer."

35. Michelle Davidson, "Case Study: Iot Lighting System Cuts Energy Costs, Improves Productivity," *Network World,* last modified July 26, 2016, https://www.networkworld.com/article/3099682/case-study-iot-lighting -system-cuts-energy-costs-improves-productivity.html.

36. "The Internet of Things Is Changing the Way We Use Energy," *Smart Grid,* accessed March 19, 2019, http://www.whatissmartgrid.org/featured-article /the-internet-of-things-is-changing-the-way-we-use-energy.

37. Peter Bendor-Samuel, "Does Your Change Management Plan Cut It in the Digital Age?" *Enterprisers Project,* last modified September 21, 2018, https://enterprisersproject.com/article/2018/9/does-your-change -management-plan-cut-it-digital-transformation-age.

CHAPTER 8: PERSONALIZATION AND THE CUSTOMER EXPERIENCE OF THE FUTURE

1. "Katrina Lake Quotes," *BrainyQuote*, accessed April 15, 2019, https://www.brainyquote.com/quotes/katrina_lake_862916.
2. "The 2017 State of Personalization Report," *Segment*, last modified October 2017, http://grow.segment.com/Segment-2017-Personalization-Report.pdf.
3. National Economic Indicator, "National, Sector, and Industry Results," *ACSI*, last modified February 2019, https://www.theacsi.org/national-economic-indicator/national-sector-and-industry-results.
4. Fareeha Ali, "A Decade in Review: Ecommerce Sales vs. Retail Sales 2007–2018," *Digital Commerce 360*, last modified February 20, 2019, https://www.digitalcommerce360.com/article/e-commerce-sales-retail-sales-ten-year-review/.
5. "2017 Connected Shoppers Report," *Sales Force Research*, last modified 2017, https://www.salesforce.com/form/industries/connected-shopper-report-2017/.
6. "The Ultimate List of 100+ Customer Experience Statistics for 2019," *Lumoame*, last modified n.d, accessed March 19, 2019, https://lumoa.me/customer-experience-stats.
7. Harshadewa, "Here's Why You Should Stop Using Personas," *UX Collective*, last modified June 2, 2018, https://uxdesign.cc/heres-why-you-should-stop-using-personas-63c09a844e67.
8. Devon McGinnis, "Customers Are Willing to Swap More Data for Personalized Marketing," *Sales Force Blog*, last modified November 4, 2016, https://www.salesforce.com/blog/2016/11/swap-data-for-personalized-marketing.html.
9. Dave Kart, "The Current State of 'Direct to Consumer' for Brand Manufacturers," *Ally Commerce*, last modified May 19, 2018, https://allycommerce.com/direct-to-consumer-brand-manufacturers/.
10. "Dollar Shave Club," *Wikipedia*, last modified March 11, 2019, https://en.wikipedia.org/wiki/Dollar_Shave_Club.
11. Omer Minkara, "The Good, the Bad, and the Ugly in Using Customer Data for Marketing," *Aberdeen*, last modified December 4, 2014, https://www.aberdeen.com/cmo-essentials/good-bad-ugly-using-customer-data-for-marketing/.
12. Minkara, "The Good, the Bad, and the Ugly in Using Customer Data for Marketing."

CHAPTER 9: THE POWER OF CUSTOMER EXPERIENCE ANALYTICS

1. "Serena Williams Quotes," *BrainyQuote*, accessed April 15, 2019 https://www.brainyquote.com/quotes/serena_williams_183397.
2. "Analytics," *Wikipedia*, last modified March 18, 2019, https://en.wikipedia.org/wiki/Analytics.
3. Mari Yamaguchi, "10 Customer Experience Statistics to Help You Plan 2019," *Genesys*, last modified November 26, 2018, https://www.genesys.com/blog/post/10-customer-experience-statistics-to-help-you-plan-2019.
4. Adrian Davis, "Not All Customers Are Created Equal," *Sales Force Blog*, last modified September 9, 2014, https://www.salesforce.com/blog/2014/09/not-all-customers-created-equal-gp.html.

5. "Customer Lifetime Value," *Wikipedia*, last modified February 26, 2019, https://en.wikipedia.org/wiki/Customer_lifetime_value.
6. Matt Ariker et al., "Personalizing at Scale," *McKinsey Insights*, last modified November 2015, https://www.mckinsey.com/business-functions/marketing-and-sales/our-insights/personalizing-at-scale.
7. Matt Ariker et al., "Personalizing at Scale."
8. Tracie Kambies et al., "Dark Analytics: Illuminating Opportunities Hidden within Unstructured Data: Tech Trends 2017," *Deloitte Insights*, last modified February 7, 2017, https://www2.deloitte.com/insights/us/en/focus/tech-trends/2017/dark-data-analyzing-unstructured-data.html.
9. Rick Whiting, "Predictive Analytics: Business Intelligence's Next Step," *CRN Magazine*, last modified May 29, 2006, https://www.crn.com/features/networking/188501302/predictive-analytics-business-intelligences-next-step.htm.
10. "Sprint Revolutionizes the Customer Experience with Pega Retention," *Pegasystems*, accessed March 19, 2019, https://www.pega.com/insights/resources/sprint-revolutionizes-customer-experience-pega-retention.
11. Vala Afshar, "Advanced Predictive Analytics and AI Will Close the Customer Experience Gap," *Huffington Post*, last modified August 22, 2017, https://www.huffingtonpost.com/entry/advanced-predictive-analytics-and-ai-will-close-the_us_599c757ae4b09dbe86ea3787.
12. Mary Shacklett, "Unstructured Data: A Cheat Sheet," *Tech Republic*, last modified July 14, 2017, https://www.techrepublic.com/article/unstructured-data-the-smart-persons-guide/.
13. Charles Babcock, "IBM Cognitive Colloquium Spotlights Uncovering Dark Data," *UBM*, last modified October 14, 2015, https://www.informationweek.com/cloud/software-as-a-service/ibm-cognitive-colloquium-spotlights-uncovering-dark-data/d/d-id/1322647.
14. "Prescriptive Analytics," *Gartner*, accessed March 19, 2019, https://www.gartner.com/it-glossary/prescriptive-analytics/.
15. Nicole Falon, "Predictive or Prescriptive Analytics? Your Business Needs Both," *Business News Daily*, last modified December 16, 2015, https://www.businessnewsdaily.com/8655-predictive-vs-prescriptive-analytics.html.
16. Amit Vij, "Casinos Bet the Future on Customer Experience and up the Ante with Analytics," *Forbes*, last modified May 31, 2018, https://www.forbes.com/sites/kinetica/2018/05/31/casinos-bet-the-future-on-customer-experience-and-up-the-ante-with-analytics/#6b1d5e2f5f9d.
17. "The Caesars Rewards Air Experience," *Caesars Enterprise Services*, accessed March 19, 2019, https://www.caesars.com/total-rewards/air.
18. Bernard Marr, "Big Data at Caesars Entertainment—a One Billion Dollar Asset?" *Forbes*, last modified May 18, 2015, https://www.forbes.com/sites/bernardmarr/2015/05/18/when-big-data-becomes-your-most-valuable-asset/#233481b31eef.
19. Kinetica, "GSK Uses Kinetica to Develop New Medicines Faster," *YouTube*, last modified December 3, 2018, https://www.youtube.com/watch?v=yQsECqghGiU.

CHAPTER 10: ETHICS AND DATA PRIVACY IN CUSTOMER EXPERIENCE

1. "Princess Margaret Quotes," BrainyQuote, accessed April 15, 2019, https://www.brainyquote.com/quotes/princess_margaret_127203.

2. Kate O'Flaherty, "Breaking Down Five 2018 Breaches—and What They Mean for Security in 2019," *Forbes*, last modified December 19, 2018, https://www.forbes.com/sites/kateoflahertyuk/2018/12/19/breaking-down-five-2018-breaches-and-what-they-mean-for-security-in-2019/#5309ee741c4f.

3. "General Data Protection Regulation," *Wikipedia*, last modified March 18, 2019, https://en.wikipedia.org/wiki/General_Data_Protection_Regulation.

4. Nicholas Confessore et al., "The Follower Factory," *New York Times*, last modified January 28, 2018, https://www.nytimes.com/interactive/2018/01/27/technology/social-media-bots.html.

5. Mary Madden and Lee Rainie, "Americans' Views About Data Collection and Security," *Pew Research Center*, last modified May 20, 2015, http://www.pewinternet.org/2015/05/20/americans-views-about-data-collection-and-security/#few-feel-they-have-a-lot-of-control-over-how-much-information-is-collected-about-them-in-daily-life.

6. "Cambridge Analytica," *Wikipedia*, last modified March 18, 2019, https://en.wikipedia.org/wiki/Cambridge_Analytica.

7. Clarke and Kinghorn, *Experience Is Everything*.

8. Jenny Darmody, "AI Can Cause Unconscious Bias—but It Could Also Be the Solution," *Silicon Republic*, last modified July 20, 2018, https://www.siliconrepublic.com/machines/alexa-gorman-inspirefest-ai-diversity.

9. Samantha Maine, "Critics Voice Concerns over Taylor Swift Installing Facial Recognition Software at Her Stadium Show," *NME*, last modified December 15, 2018, https://www.nme.com/news/music/taylor-swift-stalker-facial-recognition-cameras-2420317.

10. Karla Lant, "By 2020, There Will Be 4 Devices for Every Human on Earth," *Futurism*, last modified June 18, 2017, https://futurism.com/by-2020-there-will-be-4-devices-for-every-human-on-earth.

11. Mike O'Malley, "The 7 Craziest IoT Device Hacks," *Radware Blog*, last modified May 8, 2018, https://blog.radware.com/security/2018/05/7-craziest-iot-device-hacks/.

12. "Man Hacks Monitor, Screams at Baby Girl," *NBC News*, last modified April 28, 2014, https://www.nbcnews.com/tech/security/man-hacks-monitor-screams-baby-girl-n91546.

13. Veronica Lara, "What the Internet of Things Means for Consumer Privacy," last modified March 23, 2018, https://perspectives.eiu.com/technology-innovation/what-internet-things-means-consumer-privacy-0.

14. Fredric Paul, "People Are Really Worried About Iot Data Privacy and Security—and They Should Be," *Network World*, last modified 2018, https://www.networkworld.com/article/3267065/people-are-really-worried-about-iot-data-privacy-and-securityand-they-should-be.html.